"The sacrament of the Lord's Supper has been one of the more hotly contested topics in church history, so people in the church undoubtedly have questions about it. Dr. Keith Mathison presents a clear and biblical explanation of the Lord's Supper that will surely help people in the church to have a deeper understanding of the sacrament. He provides food for thought that both instructs and reminds us why the Lord's Supper is such a blessing for the church."

—Dr. J.V. Fesko
Professor of systematic and historical theology
Reformed Theological Seminary, Jackson, Miss.

"This is an excellent introduction to the Lord's Supper. Dr. Keith Mathison unfolds the biblical teaching, answers a range of common questions, and provides wise counsel on practical matters, including the relationship of young children to the communion service. The Reformed churches have historically attested that the supper is a means of grace. Since it is *the Lord's* Supper and in it Christ gives Himself to feed and nourish us, and because it is a proclamation of His death and communion by the Holy Spirit in His ascended humanity, it is essential to the life and vitality of the church and to its effective witness to the world. I hope that many will read Dr. Mathison's presentation and that it will be instrumental in reinvigorating the church in the years to come."

—Dr. Robert Letham
Professor of systematic and historical theology
Union School of Theology, Oxford, England

"There are many books on the Lord's Supper written by able theologians. Few address in a clear and practical way the many questions Christians have about it. Dr. Keith Mathison has answered these questions from a Reformed point of view in clear and concise language. Using church history, systematic theology, and especially biblical exegesis, Dr. Mathison shows the historical and biblical reasons for the way Reformed churches celebrate the Lord's Supper. This book is useful not only for young Christians and new believers, but also for those who have attended church for years and have never really realized what is going on during the Lord's Supper."

—DR. AUGUSTUS NICODEMUS LOPES
Vice president of Presbyterian Church of Brazil
Assistant pastor of First Presbyterian Church of Recife, Brazil

"Jesus appointed the Lord's Supper so that we would better remember Him. The Lord's Supper helps us understand the person and work of Jesus Christ and the way in which the whole of Scripture points to Christ. In the supper, believers may find refreshing streams of grace flowing from the Savior whom we meet there. In this brief and accessible book, Dr. Keith Mathison helps us better understand the Lord's Supper. Addressing biblical, theological, historical, and practical questions relating to the supper with insight and simplicity, Dr. Mathison offers readers of all levels and backgrounds a clearer understanding of the supper—and of the Savior Himself."

—DR. GUY PRENTISS WATERS
James M. Baird Jr. Professor of New Testament
Reformed Theological Seminary, Jackson, Miss.

THE
LORD'S
SUPPER

THE LORD'S SUPPER

ANSWERS TO COMMON QUESTIONS

KEITH A. MATHISON

Ⓡ *Reformation Trust*   A DIVISION OF LIGONIER MINISTRIES, ORLANDO, FL

The Lord's Supper: Answers to Common Questions
© 2019 by Keith A. Mathison

Published by Reformation Trust Publishing
a division of Ligonier Ministries
421 Ligonier Court, Sanford, FL 32771
Ligonier.org   ReformationTrust.com

Printed in Ann Arbor, Michigan
Cushing-Malloy, Inc.

0000519
First edition

ISBN 978-1-64289-135-5 (Paperback)
ISBN 978-1-64289-136-2 (ePub)
ISBN 978-1-64289-137-9 (Kindle)

Cover design: Ligonier Creative
Interior design and typeset: Katherine Lloyd, The DESK

Library of Congress Cataloging-in-Publication Data

Names: Mathison, Keith A., 1967- author.
Title: The Lord's Supper : answers to common questions / Keith A. Mathison.
Description: Orlando : Reformation Trust, 2019.
Identifiers: LCCN 2018050443 (print) | LCCN 2019013385 (ebook) | ISBN 9781642891362 (ePub) | ISBN 9781642891379 (Kindle) | ISBN 9781642891355 (pbk.)
Subjects: LCSH: Lord's Supper--Reformed Church.
Classification: LCC BX9423.C5 (ebook) | LCC BX9423.C5 M38 2019 (print) | DDC 264/.36--dc23
LC record available at https://lccn.loc.gov/2018050443

CONTENTS

INTRODUCTION

The Lord granted me faith and repentance in the year after my graduation from high school. Not long afterward, I joined a small Baptist church along with some friends who had also recently come to faith in Christ. Since I had not grown up in any church, everything was new to me. I had a lot to learn, and I was eager to do so. I read and reread the Bible, and I asked the pastor one question after another. I also made every effort to be at church during any worship service.

One of the things I noticed that our church did every month or so was observe a ceremony at the end of the worship service. The pastor would announce that we were going to observe the Lord's Supper, and after he read some words from 1 Corinthians, the deacons would distribute some thin, white, miniature crackers. They were about a half-inch across and completely tasteless, but I did not question their use. After each of us had eaten one of these, the deacons would distribute trays containing little plastic cups halfway filled with grape juice. After we drank these, the worship service would end with a hymn and an altar call.

Why did we do these things, and what did they mean? I never thought to ask. Over time, the Lord's Supper simply became part of the routine. I didn't give it a second thought. It was just something we did every once in a while.

Many years later, after moving to a different state, I found myself sitting in the new members class of a Presbyterian church. The pastor, who was teaching the class, introduced us to some of the basics of Reformed theology and Presbyterian history. We discussed the doctrines of grace, church polity, and the duties and privileges of church membership. We also discussed the sacrament of baptism at great length. A number of people in the new members class had come from Baptist churches, so the pastor wanted to make sure we understood what the Presbyterian church believed about baptism and why.

I do not recall any of our class time being devoted to the subject of the Lord's Supper. Our only exposure to the Reformed doctrine of the supper was what we read on our own time in the copies of the Westminster Confession of Faith we had been given for the class. At the time, I was focused on trying to understand the Reformed doctrine of infant baptism (a traumatic concept for those coming out of the Baptist tradition), so the doctrine of the Lord's Supper took a back seat to other issues. Since the church's actual observance of the Lord's Supper was almost identical to what I had become accustomed to in the Baptist church, that sacrament simply remained part of the routine.

I have spoken with many Christians over the years, and I do not think my experience is terribly unusual. There are many Christians sitting in the pews of churches across this nation and around the world for whom the Lord's Supper has become part of the Christian routine. They partake faithfully, and they think about Jesus while they are partaking, but they do not really understand everything that is going on during the observance of the sacrament. They do not fully understand why the pastor says certain words at various points during the supper or what those words mean. They do not fully understand why the pastor performs certain actions during the supper or what those actions mean.

If they have visited other churches, they do not understand why one church does things in one way while another church does them a different way. Why does the pastor at one church break a single loaf of bread while the pastor at another church distributes trays of mini-crackers? Why does one church use grape juice while another church uses wine? Why does one church observe the Lord's Supper every week while another church observes it monthly or quarterly?

A cursory reading of the Old Testament reveals the danger of simply going through the motions in worship without any real understanding. Such uninformed worship practices lead to a dead and deadening ritualism. Christians are to observe the Lord's Supper, but they must do so with understanding and discernment. When we begin to understand what the Lord's Supper is and what it means, when we begin to understand what God is doing and what we are doing in this sacrament, it is no longer a tedious extra fifteen minutes to endure. Instead, it is a source of great blessing, something we look forward to with anticipation.

The purpose of this book is to help Christians better understand the doctrine and practice of the Lord's Supper in the Reformed tradition. It is structured around a number of the most frequently asked questions concerning the supper. I have attempted to answer these questions in the clearest way possible. It is my prayer that readers of this book will come away from it giving glory to God for the great blessing He has given His people in this sacrament.

CHAPTER 1

WHAT IS THE LORD'S SUPPER?

Have you ever noticed the strangeness of the Lord's Supper? Many of us have been attending church for so many years that this thing we do every week or every month has become somewhat routine. Its strangeness no longer strikes us. But step back and imagine what it looks like to someone attending a church for the first time. Imagine what it looks like to a child. With some differences among churches in the details of the liturgy, the members of the church receive bread, which they eat in a ceremonial way after the pastor repeats the words of Jesus: "This is my body." Then they receive wine (or grape juice), which they ceremonially drink after the pastor repeats the words of Jesus: "This cup is the new covenant in my blood." What in the world is going on here? What is the Lord's Supper?

Scripture anticipates that the sacraments instituted by God will raise questions among believers. When the Passover was instituted, for instance, Moses said, "And when your children say to you, 'What do you mean by this service?' you shall say, 'It is the sacrifice of the LORD's Passover, for he passed over the houses of the people of Israel in Egypt, when he struck the Egyptians but spared our houses'" (Ex. 12:26–27). The Lord knew that the Passover would require explanation. He knew that Israelite children would wonder about the meaning of the rituals. We should expect nothing different when it comes to our children and the Lord's Supper. But do we know how to answer such questions? What do we say when our children ask, "What do you mean by this service?"

Christians in the Reformed tradition have studied Scripture extensively in order to answer such questions. The results of this study are found in the Reformed confessions and catechisms. The Westminster Larger Catechism, for example, provides a concise answer to the question, "What is the Lord's Supper?" "The Lord's Supper is a sacrament of the New Testament, wherein, by giving and receiving bread and wine according to the appointment of Jesus Christ, his death is showed forth; and they that worthily communicate feed upon his body and blood, to their spiritual nourishment and growth in grace; have their union and communion with him confirmed; testify and renew their thankfulness, and engagement to God, and their mutual love and fellowship each with the other, as members of the same mystical body" (WLC 168). This definition reveals how intertwined the doctrine of the Lord's Supper is with other Christian doctrines. In this catechism alone, there are 167 questions and answers before we get to the Lord's Supper, and much of what is taught in the earlier questions is assumed here. It is important, therefore, to know that our answer to the question, "What is the Lord's Supper?" cannot be understood in isolation from other Christian doctrines. It is not possible to fully grasp the Reformed doctrine of the Lord's Supper without some understanding of the doctrines of God, Scripture, sin, salvation, the incarnation, the church, and more.[1]

We see in the catechism's answer, for example, that the Lord's Supper is a sacrament. But that answer is not helpful if we do not have some idea of the nature of a sacrament. Additional problems arise because many who hear the word *sacrament* associate it with mysticism or ceremonialism. Some associate it with Roman Catholicism and cannot imagine why a Protestant church would continue to use such a loaded term. There is a fear that the use of the word might be allowing the camel's nose under the tent, and if the nose is there, the camel cannot be far behind.

This is one reason why the study of the Reformation and the confessions of the Reformation can be incredibly helpful. The Reformers had no fear of the word *sacrament* and no qualms about its continued use, and they, better than anyone today, knew the dangers of late-medieval Roman Catholicism. In addition, the Reformed churches of the following generations had no fear of the word. Almost every sixteenth- and seventeenth-century Reformed confession has a chapter titled "On the Sacraments," and Reformed theologians have used the word for centuries. As long as we define it carefully, it is a perfectly appropriate word.

How, then, is the word *sacrament* defined? The Westminster

Larger Catechism is again helpful, explaining that a sacrament is "a holy ordinance instituted by Christ in his church, to signify, seal, and exhibit unto those that are within the covenant of grace, the benefits of his mediation; to strengthen and increase their faith, and all other graces; to oblige them to obedience; to testify and cherish their love and communion one with another; and to distinguish them from those that are without" (WLC 162). The catechism goes on to explain that sacraments have two parts: a visible outward sign and the spiritual reality signified by the sign (WLC 163). Reformed churches teach that there are only two such sacraments instituted by Jesus Christ under the new covenant: baptism and the Lord's Supper.

The Lord's Supper is a sacrament of the New Testament or new covenant, instituted by Jesus Christ in the upper room on the night on which He was betrayed (Matt. 26:26–29; Mark 14:22–25; Luke 22:14–23; 1 Cor. 11:23–26). Because it is a sacrament, the Lord's Supper signifies, seals, and exhibits to believing partakers "the benefits of his [Christ's] mediation." It also strengthens and increases our faith and obliges us to obedience. It declares our love for and communion with one another as brothers and sisters in Christ. Finally, as a sacrament, the supper distinguishes those in the church from unbelievers.

What do we mean when we say that the Lord's Supper signifies, seals, and exhibits the benefits of Christ's mediation? Let us look first at the word *signifies*. Sacraments have two parts: a visible outward sign and the reality signified by that sign. In the Lord's Supper, the visible outward sign is the giving and receiving of bread and wine. The bread and wine signify Christ crucified and His benefits (WCF 29.5, 7). More specifically, the bread is the sign of Christ's body, and the wine is the sign of His blood (Matt. 26:26–28; 1 Cor. 10:16). In our day, when we hear the word *sign*, we often think of a road sign that conveys information or a symbol such as the pound sign (#, now more often known as a hashtag). This is not exactly what is meant when we refer to the bread and wine as signs of the body and blood of Christ crucified, because in the Lord's Supper there is "a spiritual relation, or sacramental union, between the sign and the thing signified" (WCF 27.2). Because of the sacramental union, a sacramental sign is distinguished from that which it signifies, but it is not separated from it. We will return to this idea of sacramental union repeatedly, so it is important to keep it in mind.

What does it mean to say that the Lord's Supper "seals" the benefits of Christ's mediation? Paul, in Romans 4:11, speaks of Abraham's circumcision as "a seal of the righteousness that he had by faith while he was still uncircumcised." The context indicates that circumcision was a seal in the sense that it confirmed the reality of the thing signified, namely, the righteousness Abraham had by faith. Circumcision authenticated it. Similarly, the Lord's Supper is a seal in the sense that it confirms and authenticates the promise of God regarding the reality of the benefits received by those who partake of the supper in faith. It indicates that the supper is no mere empty ceremony. Those who partake in faith are assured that they actually do "feed upon his body and blood, to their spiritual nourishment and growth in grace; have their union and communion with him confirmed; testify and renew their thankfulness, and engagement to God, and their mutual love and fellowship each with the other, as members of the same mystical body" (WLC 168).

Finally, what is meant by the word *exhibits*? What does it mean to say that the Lord's Supper exhibits the benefits of Christ's mediation? Again, the Westminster Confession provides a helpful place to begin thinking through the answer to this question: "The grace which is exhibited in or by the sacraments rightly used, is not conferred by any power in them; neither doth the efficacy of a sacrament depend upon the piety or intention of him that doth administer it: but upon the work of the Spirit, and the word of institution, which contains, together with a precept authorizing the use thereof, a promise of benefit to worthy receivers" (WCF 27.3). To exhibit is to hold forth. The benefits of Christ are actually held forth to believers in this sacrament. The confession here explains what this does not mean. To say that the supper exhibits the benefits of Christ's mediation does *not* mean that the bread and wine have any power in and of themselves. Furthermore, the exhibition of the benefits does not depend on the holiness or intent of the minister. It depends solely on the work of the Spirit and the promise of God found in the words of institution.

What, then, are the actual benefits? What actually does happen by the power of the Holy Spirit according to the promise of God? The Westminster Confession states: "Worthy receivers outwardly partaking of the visible elements in this sacrament, do then also, inwardly by faith, really and indeed, yet not carnally and corporally, but spiritually, receive and feed upon Christ crucified, and all benefits of His death: the body and blood of Christ being then, not corporally or carnally, in, with, or under the bread and wine; yet, as really, but spiritually, present to the faith of believers in that ordinance, as the elements themselves are to their outward senses" (WCF 29.7). We will address some of the questions that this raises in later chapters. At this point, we simply note that in the Lord's Supper, there is more going on than meets the eye. The confession points out a parallel between what is happening "outwardly" and what is happening "inwardly."

It is worth examining the main clauses before looking at the qualifying clauses lest we miss the main points. According to the confession, worthy partakers, namely, those with faith, who partake of the visible elements (bread and wine) "really and indeed . . . receive and feed upon Christ crucified, and all benefits of His death." The "body and blood of Christ" are present "to the faith of believers" as the elements of bread and wine are present "to their outward senses." The outward-inward distinction continues throughout the entire paragraph.

Clearly, the confession makes the point that this is not to be understood in some crass materialistic sense. Believers really and indeed "receive and feed upon Christ crucified" but not "carnally or corporally." This happens spiritually because the body and blood of Christ are present to the faith of believers rather than corporally or carnally present "in, with, or under the bread and wine." As the Westminster Larger Catechism puts it, "They that worthily communicate in the sacrament of

11

the Lord's Supper, do therein feed upon the body and blood of Christ, not after a corporal and carnal, but in a spiritual manner; yet truly and really, while by faith they receive and apply unto themselves Christ crucified, and all the benefits of his death" (WLC 170).

CHAPTER 2

WHAT ARE THE DIFFERENT VIEWS OF THE LORD'S SUPPER?

Most people are familiar with the doctrine of the Lord's Supper taught in their own church, but some are surprised to discover that there are other views. Some have discovered these different views through family or friends who belong to other churches. Some have read about these other views. There are differences among churches regarding both the nature of the supper and the observance of it. Historically, the fiercest debates have been those concerning the nature of the Lord's Supper, particularly the question whether and how Christ is present in the sacrament. Many of these debates center on the interpretation of Christ's words of institution. What did He mean when He said, "This is my body"? The debates came to a head during the sixteenth-century Protestant Reformation, and the views that were solidified then shape the views of the various churches today.[1]

The Roman Catholic Doctrine

The Lord's Supper, or Eucharist, is central to the liturgy of the Roman Catholic Church. It is, according to the Catechism of the Catholic Church, "the sum and summary of our faith" (section 1326). It is one of seven sacraments (along with baptism, confirmation, penance, anointing of the sick, marriage, and holy orders), and the grace that it signifies is efficaciously conferred because Christ Himself is the One who works in and through the sacrament. Therefore, the Eucharist is necessary to salvation. According to the Roman church, the elements of bread and wine become the actual body and blood of Christ when the priest pronounces the words of institution. This change in the bread and wine is known as "transubstantiation," and the doctrine was officially adopted at the Fourth Lateran Council in 1215.

The meaning of this doctrine requires a grasp of some basic concepts borrowed from Aristotle. For Aristotle, when matter and substantial form are combined, the result is a *substance*. For example, an individual chair is composed of wood (matter) and the substantial form of a chair (the form that makes it a chair rather than a table or a stool). In addition to a substantial form, the chair has qualities called *accidental forms*. Accidental forms inhere in substances giving a substance certain "accidental" qualities. These qualities are called "accidents" because they can change without causing a change in the substance of a thing. The chair can have the accidental quality of "redness," for example. If the chair is painted blue, the accidental form changes, but the substance does not change. The chair remains a chair regardless of its color.

The Roman Catholic Church adapts these basic Aristotelian metaphysical concepts in order to explain how the bread and wine can become the body and blood of Christ. According to the doctrine of transubstantiation, when the priest pronounces the words of institution, the substance of the bread and wine are miraculously changed into the substance of the body and blood of Christ. The accidents of bread and wine, however, remain. So, while the substance of the body and blood of Christ is now present, the accidents (that which we can see, touch, and taste) remain the accidents of bread and wine.

Significantly, the Roman Catholic Church also speaks of the Lord's Supper as a sacrifice. According to the Catechism of the Catholic Church, it is a sacrifice "because it *re-presents* (makes present) the sacrifice of the cross, because it is a *memorial*, and because it *applies* its fruit" (paragraph 1366, emphasis original). The sacrifice of Christ and the Eucharistic sacrifice are considered to be one and the same sacrifice (paragraph 1367), and because the church is the body of Christ, the church too is offered in this sacrifice (paragraph 1368). The doctrine of the Eucharist as a continuation, or re-presentation, of the once-for-all sacrifice of Christ and the doctrine of transubstantiation were both rejected by the Protestant Reformers.

The Lutheran Doctrine

Martin Luther rejected the Roman Catholic doctrine of transubstantiation, but he maintained belief in the real presence of Christ in the supper. Luther's view of the Lord's Supper developed during the course of controversy with Rome on one side and Andreas von Karlstadt and Huldrych Zwingli on the other. His mature view is expressed in his Large Catechism (1529). In the catechism, Luther explains that the supper "is the true body and blood of the Lord Christ in and under the bread and wine" (LC 5.8). His teaching here is based on his understanding of Christ's words of institution: "This is my body." Luther insists that to accept Christ's words is to accept the doctrine of the real presence. Any other interpretation is a denial of the truthfulness of Jesus. The promise found in Christ's words of institution, "for you" and "for the forgiveness of sins," shows us what we obtain in the sacrament (LC 5.20–22).

The Lutheran church followed Luther in his understanding of the supper. Article X of the Augsburg Confession (1530), for example, states the doctrine concisely: "It is taught among us that the true body and blood of Christ are really present in the Supper of our Lord under the form of bread and wine and are there distributed and received. The contrary doctrine is therefore rejected." Obviously, much depends on the meaning of the words "true" and "really." In the Apology of the Augsburg Confession, the meaning of these words is made clearer. The body and blood of Christ are said to be "substantially" present. The bread would not be a participation in the body of Christ (1 Cor. 10:16), it is argued, if the body of Christ were not present.

Non-Lutherans often refer to the Lutheran doctrine as "consubstantiation," a view that was suggested in the Middle Ages as an alternative to transubstantiation. According to the medieval doctrine of consubstantiation, after the words of consecration, the substance of the bread and wine remains along with (*con-*) the substance of the body and blood of Christ. This view differs from the Lutheran doctrine, however, in that it argues for the local presence of the body and blood of Christ, whereas the Lutheran view is that of a definitive or illocal presence. These are terms that are not often used today, so it is important that we understand the intended definitions. *Local* presence has to do with the way in which physical things are present. *Definitive* or *illocal* presence is the way in which finite immaterial things such as souls are present. The body of Christ born to Mary is, therefore, according to the Lutheran view, definitively or illocally present in the bread, and all who partake of the bread and wine partake of the body and blood of Christ. Those who receive it with faith partake of the blessings found in the Word of promise. Those who partake without faith incur judgment.[2]

The Reformed Doctrines

It is somewhat inaccurate to speak of *the* Reformed view of the Lord's Supper. More than one view has been represented by the various Reformed confessions and by Reformed theologians. The doctrine of Huldrych Zwingli is probably the easiest view to comprehend. He rejected the idea that the body and blood of Christ are present in any mysterious way and focused on the elements and actions of the sacrament as symbols. The Lord's Supper, according to Zwingli, is a memorial in which we remember Christ's work for us. The bread and wine are signs of His body and blood, which are present only in heaven at the right hand of God. Zwingli's view is sometimes termed "symbolic memorialism."[3]

John Calvin's view is somewhat more complex, but it is not impossible to comprehend if we understand that for him the signs and the things signified are distinguishable but also inseparable. The signs are the shadows of the heavenly reality, but the shadows are tied to the reality in the same way that the shadow of an object is inseparably tied to the object that casts the shadow. There is, then, a connection between what is found on earth during the observance of the sacrament and what is found in heaven. When a Christian partakes in faith of the bread and wine on earth, he partakes of the body and blood of Christ in the heavenly dimension. The earthly shadow shows us what is happening in the heavenly reality, in the spiritual realm. According to Calvin, we are able to partake of Christ in such a manner because of the work of the Holy Spirit who unites us to Christ.[4]

This concept helps us understand how Calvin could use the realistic language he used to speak of the Lord's Supper. It also explains the language of those later Reformed confessions that adhered more closely to Calvin's view than to Zwingli's. Article 35 of the Belgic Confession, for example, explains this parallelism in the following words when it states that Christ

has instituted an earthly and visible bread, as a sacrament of his body, and wine as a sacrament of his blood, to testify by them unto us, that, *as certainly as we receive and hold this sacrament in our hands, and eat and drink the same with our mouths, by which our life is afterwards nourished, we also do as certainly receive by faith (which is the hand and mouth of our soul) the true body and blood of Christ our only Saviour in our souls, for the support of our spiritual life.* Now, as it is certain and beyond all doubt, that Jesus Christ has not enjoined to us the use of his sacraments in vain, so he works in us all that he represents to us by these holy signs, though the manner surpasses our understanding, and cannot be comprehended by us, as the operations of the Holy Ghost are hidden and incomprehensible. In the meantime we err not, when we say, that what is eaten and drunk by us is the proper and natural body, and the proper blood of Christ. But the manner of our partaking of the same, is not by the mouth, but by the spirit through faith. (emphasis added)

According to Calvin's understanding of the Lord's Supper, the Christian's union with Christ is strengthened by his partaking of the supper in faith.[5]

Conclusion

All of these views still exist today. The Roman Catholic doctrine and the Lutheran doctrine are still represented among those churches. Over the centuries since the Reformation, Zwingli's view gradually became the majority viewpoint among

Reformed Christians. Calvin's view gradually became the minority report.[6] Newer denominations have tended to adopt views that originated among the Reformed churches. Almost all Baptist churches, for example, have adopted a symbolic memorialist view, ultimately traceable to Zwingli.[7] Pentecostalism is more difficult to assess since it is not a confessional tradition and Pentecostal churches vary widely on many doctrines. It appears, however, that most Pentecostal churches have adopted a largely Zwinglian view as well, although there is an emphasis among some Pentecostals that healing is available in this sacrament.

CHAPTER 3

WHY DID JESUS INSTITUTE THE LORD'S SUPPER ON THE PASSOVER?

The Gospels indicate that Jesus instituted the Lord's Supper on the Passover. This is clear, for example, in Matthew 26. We read in verse 17: "Now on the first day of Unleavened Bread the disciples came to Jesus, saying, 'Where will you have us prepare for you to eat the Passover?'" After hearing Jesus' answer, the disciples "prepared the Passover" (v. 19). During this Passover meal with the disciples, Jesus instituted the Lord's Supper:

> Now as they were eating, Jesus took bread, and after blessing it broke it and gave it to the disciples, and said, "Take, eat; this is my body." And he took a cup, and when he had given thanks he gave it to them, saying, "Drink of it, all of you, for this is my blood of the covenant, which is poured out for many for the forgiveness of sins. I tell you I will not drink again of this fruit of

the vine until that day when I drink it new with you in my Father's kingdom." (vv. 26–29)

But why this day? Why did Jesus not institute the Lord's Supper on some other day? Why did He choose the Passover?

To understand why Jesus instituted the Lord's Supper on this particular day, we must understand what the Passover was and what it meant to Israel. The Passover is described in the book of Exodus, which is the second book of the Pentateuch. To place the Passover in its context, however, we must take a step back and look briefly at what had happened up to that point in biblical history. We must go back to the earliest chapters of Genesis.

The first eleven chapters of Genesis recount what is often called the primeval history, from creation to the call of Abraham. Chapters 12–50 of Genesis recount the patriarchal history, from the call of Abraham to the death of Joseph in Egypt. The primeval history sets the stage for the patriarchal history by describing the desperate situation of mankind after the fall. These first eleven chapters of Genesis describe a downward spiral of sin and death. These chapters reveal why redemption is absolutely necessary. With the call of Abraham, God begins to reveal more fully how the problem of sin will be overcome and redemption accomplished.

Genesis 12–50 tells the stories of Abraham, Isaac, Jacob, and Joseph. These chapters begin with the call of Abraham and the establishment of the Abrahamic covenant. In this covenant, God promises Abraham that he will become a great nation and that he will be given the land of Canaan. God also promises that through Abraham's seed all the families of the earth shall be blessed (Gen. 12:3). These covenant promises to Abraham are confirmed to each succeeding patriarch. However, in Genesis 15:13, God reveals to Abraham that his descendants will be afflicted in a foreign land for four hundred years. But God also promises salvation. In Genesis 50:24, Joseph speaks to his brothers in Egypt, telling them that God will deliver them and bring them to the land He promised to Abraham, Isaac, and Jacob (cf. 46:4). Genesis, therefore, anticipates the great act of redemption described in the book of Exodus.

As the book of Exodus begins, Israel has been in Egypt for more than four hundred years (cf. Ex. 12:40). They are now in bondage under an oppressive Pharaoh. The early chapters of Exodus describe the calling of Moses to be the one who will lead God's people out of slavery in Egypt. He comes before Pharaoh demanding that Israel be allowed to go and worship the Lord, but Pharaoh refuses. God then sends a series of increasingly severe plagues on Egypt. Pharaoh's stubbornness in the face of the first nine plagues results in God's pronouncement of a final plague that will result in Israel's redemption from slavery. God warns that He will go into the midst of Egypt and that every firstborn in the land will die. It is in the context of the warning of this final plague that we find God's instructions regarding the Passover in Exodus 12.

God begins with a statement indicating that the Passover and Exodus will mark a new beginning for the nation of Israel. The month of Abib (late March and early April) is to be the first month of the year for God's people. This emphasizes the fact that the exodus from Egypt is a key event, a turning point, in redemptive history. So central is the event that from this point forward, God is frequently described in reference to the exodus (e.g., Ex. 20:2; Lev. 11:45; Num. 15:41; Deut. 5:6; Josh. 24:17; Judg. 6:8; 1 Sam. 10:18; 2 Kings 17:36; Ps. 81:10; Jer. 11:4; Dan. 9:15; Hos. 11:1; Amos 2:10). He is identified as the One who redeemed His people from slavery.[1]

In later years, the observation of the Passover would involve the priesthood (cf. Deut. 16:5–7), but on the night of the original Passover, the responsibility for this ceremony falls to the head of each household. The head of every household is commanded to take a male lamb that is one year old and without any blemishes. This substitutionary lamb must be a symbol of perfection. As such, it foreshadows the true Lamb of God, Jesus Christ, who was uniquely without blemish (cf. 1 Peter 1:19). At twilight, the lamb for each household is to be killed.

The Lord then reveals what the Israelites are to do with the slain lambs and why they are to do it. Each head of a household is to take the blood of the lamb and put it on the doorposts and lintel of his house. God explains that the blood will be a sign. When He sees the blood on the door, He will pass over that house, and the firstborn in it will be spared from the coming judgment that is to fall on Egypt. After the lambs are killed by the head of the household, they are to be roasted and eaten with the people dressed and prepared to leave on a moment's notice. Since the Passover is a "sacrifice" (cf. Ex. 12:27; 34:25; Deut. 16:2), the eating of the lamb is a sacrificial meal like that associated with the peace offering described in Leviticus 3 and 7. In such meals, the body of the sacrificial victim is offered to believers to eat after the sacrifice is made (Lev. 7:15).

In Exodus 12:14–20, God reveals the way future generations of Israelites are to observe the Passover. The exodus from Egypt is to be commemorated in the seven-day Feast of Unleavened Bread, which will be commenced with the Passover observance. The people are always to remember their slavery in Egypt and God's act of redemption in freeing them from this bondage. The Passover, therefore, is to be observed throughout their generations.

Exodus 12:21–28 contains Moses' instructions to the people regarding the Passover and the people's response. Moses instructs the people to mark the doors using hyssop, a plant that will later be used in connection with various purification rituals (cf. Lev. 14:49–52; Num. 19:18–19). Although some scholars have denied that the Passover is a sacrifice, Moses specifically refers to it as such in Exodus 12:27. Although no specific sin is mentioned, the blood of the lamb turns away the wrath of God. Here again the Passover foreshadows the redemptive work of Christ (1 Cor. 5:7).

The tenth and final plague comes on Egypt just as God warned through Moses and Aaron, and the firstborn throughout the land are struck dead. Only those covered by the blood of the lamb are spared. As a result of this final plague, Pharaoh finally relents and commands Moses and the Israelites to go. The beginning of the exodus itself is described in Exodus 12:33–42. The reason for God's instructions to be prepared to leave in haste now becomes clear. The Egyptians want the Israelites out immediately and urge them to depart. The Israelites plunder the Egyptians of their silver and gold, and after 430 years, they begin the journey out of Egypt and toward the promised land.

Our brief survey of Exodus 12 reveals several important facts about the Passover. The blood of the Passover lamb distinguished the people of God from the unbelieving Egyptians, and observation of the Passover was a sign of faith in God. The Passover also marked Israel's redemption from slavery in Egypt. It commemorated her birth as a nation. Throughout all of Israel's generations, the Passover was to be a memorial of God's great redemptive act. It was also to be a teaching opportunity for Israelite parents, who were to explain its significance to their children.

In the later prophetic books of the Old Testament, the exodus would be viewed as the paradigmatic act of redemption. When the prophets looked toward God's future work of redemption, they compared it to the original exodus and spoke of it in terms of a new and greater exodus. We see such language, for example, in Isaiah 52:11–12, where God commanded Israel to depart from Babylon using language reminiscent of that used in connection with the original exodus from Egypt. At the close of the Old Testament, the Israelites were looking forward to a new and greater exodus.

When the Gospels open, it is no coincidence that numerous parallels are seen between Jesus and Moses and between Jesus and Israel.[2] Jesus was even taken down into Egypt only to return after the death of Herod. This is said to have occurred "to fulfill what the Lord had spoken by the prophet, 'Out of Egypt I called my son'" (Matt. 2:15). Herod's decree to kill all the male children in Bethlehem is a gruesome echo of Pharaoh's decree to kill all the male children of the Israelites (Matt. 2:16; cf. Ex. 1:15–22). Commentators discuss even more parallels, but the point of the parallels is to communicate to the reader that the long-awaited time of redemption was at hand. The prophesied new exodus was near.

Why, then, did Jesus institute the Lord's Supper on the Passover the night before His crucifixion? In the first place, it is because He is the fulfillment of all that was foreshadowed by the Passover lamb. His blood, the blood of the new covenant, averts the wrath of God for those who place their faith in Him. Second, it is because the Last Supper was the eve of the prophesied greater new covenant act of redemption—the promised act of redemption that the prophets described in terms of a new exodus—and just as the first exodus was preceded by the institution of the Passover, the greater new exodus was preceded by the institution of the Lord's Supper. Jesus instituted the Lord's Supper on this night to signify that this new exodus was about to begin. This act indicated that the time of redemption had come.

CHAPTER 4

WHAT DID JESUS MEAN WHEN HE SAID, "THIS IS MY BODY" AND "THIS IS MY BLOOD OF THE COVENANT"?

Jesus' words of institution on the night He was betrayed are a major bone of contention among proponents of different views of the Lord's Supper. All sides in the debate desire to understand what Jesus intended with His words, but what exactly did He intend when He said, "This is my body" and "This is my blood of the covenant"? Was He speaking literally? Was He speaking figuratively? Was He doing something else altogether? These are not simple questions to answer, but they are important. Let us look at each of His statements in turn.

This Is My Body

Few statements in Scripture have been the source of more controversy and disagreement than Jesus' words "This is my body" (Matt. 26:26; Mark 14:22; Luke 22:19). In some traditions, such as Roman Catholicism, Eastern Orthodoxy, and Lutheranism, Jesus' words are interpreted in a more or less literal manner. Christians in other traditions interpret the words figuratively to one degree or another. According to many Roman Catholics and Lutherans, interpreting Jesus' words in anything less than a strictly literal manner betrays a lack of faith in the truthfulness of God's Word. According to these traditions, the words "This is my body" can mean only one thing, namely, that the bread, somehow and in some way, literally *is* Jesus' body.

A few moments' reflection, however, reveals that the words "This is" do not always require a strictly literal identification. A phrase with the structure "This is that" can be used in a number of different contexts with varying degrees of connection between the subject and the predicate. Imagine, for example, that you are standing with your father and you introduce him to someone, saying, "This is my father." Here we see a very literal use of the words. Now imagine showing someone a photograph of your father while saying, "This is my father." Because the piece of paper with the image on it is not literally your father (it did not beget you), the words "This is" are being used in a less than strictly literal manner.

Now imagine standing in a room with people and pointing to a live television broadcast of your father while saying to the people present, "This is my father." Here, there is a stronger connection between the image and the reality than there is between the photograph and the real person because you are seeing something that is really happening somewhere. But the image on the television screen is still not literally your father. Your father and the image on the screen are distinguishable realities. One is a flesh-and-blood individual; the other is a collection of pixels.

Using a different example, one could also imagine an instance in which you pointed to a paper cup and said, "This is my soda." Your soda is *in* the paper cup, but the paper cup is not literally your soda. You are saying, "This *is* my soda," while pointing to something that *contains* your soda. All of this may seem pedantic, but it is important to make the point, and the point is simply this: the words "This is" can be used in a variety of ways, not all of which indicate strict identity. Only the context in which the words are used can determine whether such a statement is intended literally.

What then was the context in which Jesus' declaration was made? The context was a Passover meal. Why is this important? In the Passover meal there were several kinds of food that were understood to be symbolic of something else. The one presiding at the meal explained the symbolism of these foods to those present. Because it was a Passover meal, those attending fully expected to hear symbolic explanations of the food items as part of the standard Jewish liturgy. In the context of a Passover meal, such words would not come as a surprise.

Because of this context, when the one officiating said about the bread, "*This is* the bread of affliction *which our ancestors ate* when they came from the land of Egypt," it would have never occurred to anyone present that the bread was literally "transformed" or "changed" into the exact same pieces of bread their ancestors ate and digested centuries before. It would never have occurred to anyone that the "accidents" were *this* bread, while the "substance" was *that* bread. Under what conceivable circumstance would anyone have thought that the bread their ancestors ate and digested was somehow "in, with, or under" the bread they were eating in the present time? The liturgy called for explanations of the symbolic food, and that is how those present understood it. Transubstantiation, consubstantiation, and all other such concepts built on a woodenly literal interpretation of Jesus' words are completely alien to the symbolic Passover context.

When Jesus picked up the bread, the disciples present expected to hear the familiar words, "This is the bread of affliction." Instead Jesus broke the bread and said, "This is my body, which is given for you" (Luke 22:19). He was still explaining the symbolism of the food, but in light of the new covenant, the symbolism had changed. Jesus identified that which had been symbolic of affliction with His own body. It had formerly symbolized the affliction of the old Israel. Now it symbolized the affliction of the new Israel, Jesus Christ. It anticipated His imminent atoning death. When we compare the words spoken about the bread with the words spoken about the wine ("poured out for many"; Matt. 26:28), this association with death is confirmed. He would be afflicted and die for the sins of His people (Isa. 53:4, 7).

This Is My Blood of the Covenant

The interpretation of Jesus' words about the cup is closely connected to the interpretation of His words about the bread. As we observed in our discussion of the bread, these words were spoken in the context of a Passover meal in which food items had a symbolic significance that was explained by the one presiding. Those attending the meal fully expected to hear symbolic explanations of the food items as part of the standard Jewish liturgy. As we have also observed, the words "This is" do not require a woodenly literal interpretation, and we would certainly not expect such in the context of a symbolic meal like the Passover. There is no reason, then, to conclude that Jesus intended to say that the wine was somehow transformed into His literal blood or that His literal blood was in, with, or under the wine.

If Jesus did not mean to say that the wine is somehow literally His own blood, what did He mean? Wine was sometimes associated with blood in the Old Testament (e.g., Gen. 49:11; Deut. 32:14; Isa. 63:3, 6), but that does not help us fully understand what Jesus is saying. To understand the meaning of Jesus' words, it may help to see which part of His words each gospel author chose to emphasize.

Drink of it, all of you, for this is my blood of the covenant, which is poured out for many for the forgiveness of sins. (Matt. 26:27–28)	This is my blood of the covenant, which is poured out for many. (Mark 14:24)	This cup that is poured out for you is the new covenant in my blood. (Luke 22:20)

All three gospel authors recount Jesus' words about "my blood" being "poured out." When the words "my blood" are used in the Old Testament, death is usually the meaning involved. When the words "my blood" are found with "poured out," violent death is often in view, sometimes in reference to a bloody sacrifice.

The words "for many" or "for you" allude to the prophecy found in Isaiah 53:10–12. There Isaiah speaks of the Suffering Servant's making "many to be accounted righteous" and bearing "the sin of many." Moses had said many years before that "it is the blood that makes atonement" (Lev. 17:11). Jesus accomplished our atonement through His death on the cross, through the pouring out of His blood. Matthew adds that the pouring out of Jesus' blood (i.e., His death) is "for the forgiveness of sins." This too ties Jesus' words to Isaiah 53, specifically verses 5–12, where the Suffering Servant is said to be "pierced for our transgressions" and "crushed for our iniquities." He "makes an offering for guilt" and bears sin.

All three gospel authors recount Jesus' use of the word "covenant" in the context of the Last Supper. Matthew and Mark use the phrase "blood of the covenant," while Luke uses the phrase "new covenant in my blood." The specific phrase "blood of the covenant" alludes to Exodus 24:8 and the account of the ratification of the Sinai covenant by Moses. At Mount Sinai, Moses took the sacrificial blood and threw it on the people. Then he said, "Behold the blood of the covenant that the LORD has made with you in accordance with all these words." Jesus' words indicate that His blood, like the sacrificial blood at Sinai, ratified a covenant. Luke's use of the phrase "new covenant" indicates that the covenant Jesus was ratifying through His death is the new covenant prophesied in Jeremiah 31:31–34.

It is important to hear Jesus' words about the bread and wine in their own biblical context. When we read these words in the light of the first-century Passover context, we understand that they were spoken in the context of a meal that involved the explanations of foods with symbolic meanings. We realize that certain questions that arose later in the history of the church regarding the meaning of these words missed the point entirely. Such questions would not have even made sense to the disciples at the Passover.

CHAPTER 5

WHAT DOES PAUL TEACH CONCERNING THE LORD'S SUPPER IN 1 CORINTHIANS 10–11?

Outside of the Gospels, the most substantial discussion of the Lord's Supper is found in the tenth and eleventh chapters of Paul's first epistle to the Corinthians. These chapters raise almost as many questions as Jesus' words of institution in the Gospels. What does Paul mean in 1 Corinthians 10 when he says that the bread and wine are a "participation" in the body and blood of Christ? What does he mean in 1 Corinthians 11 when he says that in eating the Lord's Supper we "proclaim the Lord's death until he comes"? What does it mean to "discern the body" of Christ? We will address each of these questions in turn.

1 Corinthians 10

Paul's comment about the bread and the wine's being a "participation" in the body and blood of Christ is found in 1 Corinthians 10 at the end of a lengthy argument concerning the eating of food offered to idols. This argument begins in chapter 8 and concludes in chapter 10. In chapter 8, Paul reminds the Corinthians that idols have no real existence and that there is only one true God (vv. 4–6). Not everyone knows this, however, so some eat food thinking it really has been offered to an idol. In doing so, their conscience is defiled (v. 7). Those who do know the truth about idols are warned not to let their knowledge cause the weak to stumble. It is better not to eat such meat than to cause a brother to stumble (vv. 8–13).

In chapter 9, Paul offers his own practice as an example to the Corinthians. Then, in chapter 10, he turns to the danger of idolatry. In verses 1–13, Paul argues that what happened to Israel as a result of her sins was written down for our instruction. They were idolaters. They were sexually immoral. They put Christ to the test. They grumbled. Christians are not to do any of these things. In verses 14–22, Paul moves to the implication of all he has said thus far by urging the Corinthians to flee idolatry (v. 14). What they know about the Lord's Supper (v. 16) and the Old Testament sacrificial meals (v. 18) should be sufficient to convince them that eating food sacrificed to idols is idolatry (vv. 19–21). To partake of the Lord's Supper precludes one from partaking of food offered to idols.

Paul specifically refers to the Lord's Supper in 10:16 when he says: "The cup of blessing that we bless, is it not a participation in the blood of Christ? The bread that we break, is it not a participation in the body of Christ?" These comments are introduced as the foundation for what he will say in the following verses about food offered to idols, so the Lord's Supper is not the primary focus of this passage. However, what Paul says about the supper here is significant. What does he mean when he speaks of the wine and bread as a "participation" in the blood and body of Christ?

The word translated "participation" is the Greek word *koinōnia*. The meaning of the word in this context is disputed. According to some interpreters, Paul is speaking of participation with Christ Himself. According to others, he is speaking of participation with other believers who are observing the sacrament. In fact, both are involved. In verse 17, the vertical dimension of communion with Christ is the foundation of the horizontal communion in the fellowship of the church: "Because there is one bread, we who are many are one body, for we all partake of the one bread."

In verse 18, Paul uses the Old Testament sacrificial meals to illuminate what he means by the word "participation." He writes: "Consider the people of Israel: are not those who eat the sacrifices participants in the altar?" This is significant because it means that if we want to understand what Paul means when he speaks of the bread and wine as participation in the body and blood of Christ, we must understand what he means when he speaks of Old Testament Israel as "participants in the altar" whenever they ate the sacrifices.

To understand what Paul is saying here, it is necessary to

understand something of the nature of Old Testament sacrificial meals. One of the most helpful explanations of these meals is found in a short article by Benjamin B. Warfield titled "The Fundamental Significance of the Lord's Supper."[1] Warfield argues that the most important fact about the Lord's Supper is that it was instituted during the Passover meal. He argues that the Lord's Supper is exactly what the Passover was—a sacrificial meal. In such meals, the sacrifice was eaten by the people after it was offered to God. Sacrificial meals were an application of the sacrifice to the people and were thus the people's "participation in the altar."[2] Those who partook of the meal participated in the benefits obtained in the sacrifice itself.

As Warfield goes on to explain, those who partake of the new symbols of Christ (the bread and wine) partake of the One who was offered on the cross as a sacrifice for sin just as Old Testament Israelites partook of the animal that had *already* been sacrificed. Warfield explains: "The sacrificial feast is not the sacrifice, in the sense of the act of offering: it is, however, the sacrifice, in the sense of the thing offered, that is eaten in it."[3] In other words, the participants in the supper appropriate the reality and the benefits that the sacrifice represents and accomplishes, but they do not carry out the *act* of sacrifice itself. In any sacrificial meal, the act of sacrifice is necessarily already accomplished.

Paul's mention of the Old Testament saints in 1 Corinthians 10:18 clarifies for us what he means when he speaks of participation in the body and blood of Christ. Just as the Old Testament saints partook of the Passover lamb after it had been sacrificed, New Testament believers partake of Christ our Passover Lamb. We partake not only of Christ Himself but also of the benefits of His sacrificial death on the cross. This is why believers cannot eat food offered to idols in the pagan temples. To do so indicates willing participation in that sacrifice, and since that act of sacrifice was made to demonic beings, participation in that sacrifice amounts to idolatry.

Although we partake of Christ, can Paul's words be used to support a Roman Catholic or Lutheran interpretation of the bread and wine? No. Paul speaks of partaking of bread and wine as "participation in" the body and blood of Christ (v. 16). But two verses later in the same context, he also speaks of the Old Testament saints who ate the sacrifices as "participants in the altar." The two statements inform each other. If the first must be interpreted in the Roman Catholic or Lutheran sense of "transubstantiation" or "real presence," so too must the other. If the second cannot be interpreted in the Roman Catholic or Lutheran sense, then it is inconsistent to assert that the first must be interpreted in such a sense.

To my knowledge, no one has ever argued that when Paul said Old Testament Israelites were "participants in the altar" he intended to teach the "real presence" of the altar in the Old Testament sacrifices. No one has argued that he intended to teach that the Old Testament sacrifices were transubstantiated into the altar. In other words, "participation in the altar" by those who ate the Old Testament sacrifices does not mean and cannot possibly mean anything approaching the Roman Catholic or Lutheran doctrine. But if no one disputes the meaning of this text, the implication is that it is necessarily clearer and therefore should be allowed to shed light on what Paul means when in the same context he uses the same language regarding participation in the body and blood of Christ.

1 Corinthians 11

In 1 Corinthians 11, Paul addresses the subject of the Lord's Supper explicitly because of abuses that were taking place in the observance of the supper in the church at Corinth. In verses 17–22, Paul informs the Corinthians that he had heard of the divisions among them, and he had heard of how these divisions affected their observance of the Lord's Supper. Apparently, the church was following the customs of the locals, and the host was keeping the best food for himself and his wealthier guests. The leftovers were going to those from the lower levels of society. Paul is highly critical of the Corinthians for this.

In verses 23–26, Paul reminds the Corinthians of what the Lord's Supper was originally intended to be. He first reminds them of the words of institution spoken by Christ on the night He was betrayed. Paul then says: "For as often as you eat this bread and drink the cup, you proclaim the Lord's death until he comes" (v. 26). What does Paul mean by this? The word translated "proclaim" is usually used in the New Testament in the context of proclaiming the gospel. Here Paul is saying that when the Lord's Supper is observed, the Lord's death is proclaimed.

Some believe the supper itself is the proclamation. In other words, the supper is an "acted sermon." Others argue that the proclamation is a verbal message that occurs during the meal. Either way, the basic point is that the observance of the Lord's Supper is the occasion for testifying to the great work of redemption accomplished by Jesus on the cross. In any other context, proclaiming someone's death "until he comes" would make no sense, but the Lord did not remain dead. He is now risen, and one day He will return.

The words "until he comes" look forward to the second coming of Jesus. These words point to the eschatological element of the Lord's Supper. Not only does the supper look back ("Do this in remembrance of me"), but it also looks forward to the consummation, giving us a foretaste of the Supper of the Lamb (Rev. 19:9). These words place the church in the time between the times, indicating that the church has not reached its final destination yet. This was an important point to make to the Corinthians, whose overrealized eschatology led them to believe that there was nothing more to come.

In 1 Corinthians 11:27–29, Paul warns the Corinthians about eating and drinking in an unworthy manner. To do so is to profane the body and blood of the Lord (v. 27). It is for this reason that believers must examine themselves before partaking of the supper (v. 28). Paul writes, "For anyone who eats and drinks without discerning the body eats and drinks judgment on himself" (v. 29). What does Paul mean when he speaks of "discerning the body"? The most common interpretation in the history of the church is that Paul is speaking of Christians' distinguishing between the consecrated elements and ordinary bread and wine. In other words, his statement has to do with understanding that there is a real sacramental union between the signs and the things signified. The use of the words "body" and "blood" in the immediate context (vv. 24–25, 27) lend support to this interpretation.

Another interpretation is that "discerning the body" refers to our realizing that the church is the body of Christ. Paul does describe the church as the body of Christ in the same book (10:17), and the problem he is addressing in chapter 11 has to do with Christians' disturbing the unity of the church in the divisive way they are practicing the Lord's Supper (11:18–22). The two interpretations are not mutually exclusive. It appears likely that Paul's use of the phrase "discerning the body" in 11:29 has both ideas in mind since both ideas have already been conjoined by him in 10:16–17. If we discern that the bread and wine are signs of the body and blood of Christ and that those signs are in a sacramental union with the reality they signify, we will not do anything to rend the ecclesiastical body of Christ, especially in our partaking of the supper.

CHAPTER 6

IS JESUS PRESENT
IN THE LORD'S SUPPER?

For many, to ask whether Christ is present in the Lord's Supper is absurd. Did Jesus not say that where two or three are gathered in His name, there He would be among them (Matt. 18:20)? Did He not say that He would be with His disciples always (Matt. 28:20)? Yes He did, and yes He is, but this question is asking something more specific. In the history of the church, one of the most controversial issues has been the nature of Christ's presence in the sacrament of the Lord's Supper. Specifically, are the body and blood of Christ present in the elements of bread and wine, and if so, how? Are the bread and wine transubstantiated into the body and blood of Christ? Are the body and blood of Christ present in, with, or under the bread and wine? Is Christ "spiritually" present, and if so, what exactly does that mean? How would a spiritual presence differ from omnipresence?

In order to answer such questions, we must take a step

back and look at what Scripture teaches regarding the person of Christ. When we read the Gospels, we notice that Jesus says and does things that only a true man could say and do. He hungers and thirsts (Mark 11:12; John 19:28). He grows weary (John 4:6). More significantly, He suffers and dies (Mark 8:31). We also notice that this same Jesus says and does things that only one who is truly God could say and do. He forgives sins (Mark 2:10). He hears prayer and accepts worship (Matt. 21:16; John 14:13–14; Acts 7:59). He claims equality with the Father (John 5:17–29). He claims to have been with the Father before the world existed (John 17:5). How could one and the same person say and do all of these things? What are we to make of this biblical witness to Christ? That was the question the early church faced as it attempted to answer the questions that were asked both by new believers and by outsiders.

As the church wrestled with the scriptural teaching, numerous wrong answers arose. These false doctrines were ultimately rejected as heresy because they did not do justice to the fullness of biblical teaching. They ignored one or more major elements of biblical doctrine. The Nicene Creed of AD 325 was a landmark in the process of stating concisely the fullness of what the Bible teaches about the Lord Jesus Christ. Arian and gnostic views of the Trinity were rejected, and Jesus was declared to be *homoousios* with the Father. In other words, the Son was said to be God in the same sense that the Father is God. The Niceno-Constantinopolitan Creed of AD 381 clarified the same teaching, stating that Jesus is "God from God, Light from

Light, true God from true God, begotten, not made; of the same essence as the Father." So, by the end of the fourth century, the church had stated clearly that Jesus is truly God.

But how does one who is truly God hunger and thirst and suffer and die? That question continued to cause controversy. One group of teachers taught what has come to be known as a "two sons" doctrine. They granted that Jesus is truly God and truly man, but they distinguished these two natures to the point of separation, a separation that would not allow them to meaningfully identify the Son of Mary with the Son of God (thus two sons). This view maintained the reality of the two natures, but it did so at the cost of destroying the unity of Christ. The Nestorian controversy was the culmination of the debates that arose as a result of this teaching. Another way of solving the problem was to blur or blend the two natures into some new third thing that was neither truly human nor truly divine. This solution, associated with Eutyches, maintained the unity of Christ, but it did so at the cost of denying Christ's true divinity and true humanity.

The church's solution to the problem was ultimately formulated at the Council of Chalcedon in AD 451. In the penultimate paragraph, the council provided a concise statement that did justice to the fullness of the biblical teaching. It reads as follows:

> So, following the saintly fathers, we all with one voice teach the confession of one and the same Son, our Lord Jesus Christ: the same perfect in divinity and perfect in

humanity, the same truly God and truly man, of a rational soul and a body; consubstantial with the Father as regards his divinity, and the same consubstantial with us as regards his humanity; like us in all respects except for sin; begotten before the ages from the Father as regards his divinity, and in the last days the same for us and for our salvation from Mary, the virgin God-bearer as regards his humanity; one and the same Christ, Son, Lord, only-begotten, acknowledged in two natures which undergo no confusion, no change, no division, no separation; at no point was the difference between the natures taken away through the union, but rather the property of both natures is preserved and comes together into a single person and a single subsistent being; he is not parted or divided into two persons, but is one and the same only-begotten Son, God, Word, Lord Jesus Christ, just as the prophets taught from the beginning about him, and as the Lord Jesus Christ himself instructed us, and as the creed of the fathers handed it down to us.

The repeated words "one and the same" and "the same" emphasize that Christ is a single person, the single subject of all that is said about Him in Scripture and in the Nicene Creed. He is one person with two natures (divine and human). The two natures are united in the one person of Christ without confusion or change and without division or separation. The properties, or attributes, of both natures are preserved.

All of this is important because when the question of Christ's presence in the Lord's Supper is raised, the Nicene Creed and the Definition of Chalcedon are doctrinal statements confessed by all parties in the debate. If this Niceno-Chalcedonian doctrine concerning the person of Christ is an agreed-upon starting point, it should rule out certain answers. It would rule out, for example, any answer that explicitly or implicitly denies the true deity or true humanity of Christ. It would rule out any answer that explicitly or implicitly confuses, changes, divides, or separates the natures of Christ. Finally, it would rule out any answer that explicitly or implicitly denies the preservation of the properties of the two natures.

Returning to the biblical statements about Christ, we see that Jesus said He would be with His disciples always (Matt. 28:20). Yet, He also tells the disciples: "It is to your advantage that I go away, for if I do not go away, the Helper will not come to you. But if I go, I will send him to you" (John 16:7). Because Christ is truly God, He has the divine attribute of omnipresence. There is no place where the divine nature is not present. But because Christ is also truly man, "consubstantial with us as regards his humanity," He has a truly human body and soul. A truly human body is finite. It can be in one place but not another. Regarding His body, it was said, "He is not here, for he has risen" (Matt. 28:6). We can say with all confidence that there is at least one place that the body of Christ is not present, and that is the tomb in which He was buried. His body is *not* there, for He is risen.

If we can say of Christ's body that it is not in the tomb, then His body is not omnipresent. If His body is not in the grave, it cannot be unbiblical in principle to deny the presence of Christ's body in a particular place. We can say, for example, that His body is not now present on earth. Where is Christ's human body? Since the ascension, His human body is in heaven. The Nicene Creed uses the language "seated at the right hand of God." From heaven, He will come again with glory to judge the living and the dead. When the Bible and our creeds use language that speaks of Christ's being in one place and not in another or language indicating movement from earth to heaven (Acts 1:6–11) or from heaven to earth (1 Thess. 4:16), they are speaking of His finite human body. They are speaking in terms of properties that apply specifically to the finite human body of Christ—properties that have been preserved even after the hypostatic union.

It is because of our belief that Christ has a true human body that is of the same nature as our human bodies that we reject any view that implies otherwise. We reject the view that affirms that the bread transforms into the body of Christ, and we reject those views that affirm that His body is corporeally eaten with the mouth when the bread is eaten. Such views either explicitly or implicitly deny that the body of Christ retains its true human properties. They deny that His body is a truly human body. We cannot confess with Chalcedon the biblical teaching that the "property of both natures is preserved" while at the same time attributing the divine property of omnipresence to the human body of Christ. Our interpretation of Christ's words "This is my body" cannot be interpreted in a way that effectively denies the true humanity of Christ.

The Westminster Confession of Faith states that while the body and blood of Christ are not "corporally or carnally, in, with, or under the bread and wine," they are "as really, but spiritually, present to the faith of believers in that ordinance, as the elements themselves are to their outward senses" (29.7). This is a denial of any kind of presence that would effectively nullify the true human nature of Christ, any kind of presence that would have His body physically present in multiple places at once. It is an affirmation, on the other hand, of what the confession terms a real and spiritual presence.

Note first that the body and blood are said to be as really present as the elements of bread and wine themselves. However, although they are just as really present as the bread and wine, they are known to be present in a different manner. The elements of bread and wine are known to be present through our "outward senses." We can see and smell and taste the bread and wine. The body and blood of Christ are known to be present not through our outward senses but through our faith.

The confession uses the word "spiritually" to describe the nature of this presence. The word "spiritually" can easily be misunderstood. The confession is not saying that only Jesus' "spirit" is present. It clearly speaks of the presence of His body and blood, not merely the presence of His spirit. The word "spiritually" has to do with the manner of the presence. This presence of the body and blood of Christ that we know through faith comes about by the work of the Holy Spirit. It is the Spirit who makes real the connection, the sacramental union, between the signs and the things signified. Thus, it is by the work of the Spirit that Christians "inwardly by faith, really and indeed, yet not carnally and corporally but spiritually, receive, and feed upon, Christ crucified" when they outwardly partake of the visible elements.

CHAPTER 7

IS THE LORD'S SUPPER A SACRIFICE?

I n the Roman Catholic Church, the Lord's Supper, or Eucharist, is referred to as the sacrifice of the Mass. According to the Roman Catholic Church, this means that the Lord's Supper is a re-presentation of the sacrifice of Christ. In 1562, the twenty-second session of the Council of Trent dogmatically defined the doctrine of the sacrifice of the Mass. Chapter 1 of the twenty-second session explains that before Christ our High Priest offered Himself, He left His church a visible sacrifice in order that His priesthood might not come to an end. The visible sacrifice would represent the bloody sacrifice He was to offer once on the cross. This visible sacrifice would keep the memory of the bloody sacrifice in the memory of the church and apply its benefits that our sins might be remitted. According to the Council of Trent, at the Last Supper, Christ "offered up to God the Father His own body and blood under the form of bread and wine."[1] He commanded His Apostles whom He had made priests to do the same.

Chapter 2 explains that because the sacrifice of the Mass contains in an unbloody manner the same Christ who offered Himself in a bloody manner, this unbloody sacrifice is "truly propitiatory." In other words, it appeases God, and He forgives the sins of penitent believers who partake of this sacrament. Furthermore, this sacrifice can be offered for the sins of both the living and the dead.[2] The remaining chapters go on to explain various elements regarding the ceremonies associated with the sacrifice of the Mass. The canons that follow anathematize those who do not believe this doctrine to be biblical. The first five canons focus more on the doctrinal issues at hand:

Canon 1. If anyone says that in the mass a true and real sacrifice is not offered to God; or that to be offered is nothing else than that Christ is given to us to eat, let him be anathema.

Canon 2. If anyone says that by those words, Do this for a commemoration of me, Christ did not institute the Apostles priests; or did not ordain that they and other priests should offer His own body and blood, let him be anathema.

Canon 3. If anyone says that the sacrifice of the mass is one only of praise and thanksgiving; or that it is a mere commemoration of the sacrifice consummated on the cross but not a propitiatory one; or that it profits him only who receives, and ought not to be offered for the living and the dead, for sins, punishments, satisfactions, and other necessities, let him be anathema.

Canon 4. If anyone says that by the sacrifice of the mass a blasphemy is cast upon the most holy sacrifice of Christ consummated on the cross; or that the former derogates from the latter, let him be anathema.

Canon 5. If anyone says that it is a deception to celebrate masses in honor of the saints and in order to obtain their intercession with God, as the Church intends, let him be anathema.[3]

These canons and decrees of the Council of Trent are official dogma of the Roman Catholic Church. These are doctrines that all Roman Catholics must believe.

The Council of Trent was called as a response to the teaching of the Protestant Reformers. All of the first-generation Reformers had rejected the doctrine of the sacrifice of the Mass. In his 1520 work *The Babylonian Captivity of the Church*, Martin Luther referred to the sacrifice of the Mass as "the most wicked abuse of all."[4] The main problem, in Luther's mind, was that the Roman doctrine turned the sacrament into a work. He argued that the supper is a promise to be received by faith.[5] In his Sixty-Seven Articles, written in 1523, Huldrych Zwingli also rejected the Roman doctrine, saying, "The mass is not a sacrifice, but a memorial of the sacrifice and a seal of the redemption which Christ has manifested to us."[6] John

Calvin referred to the Roman Catholic doctrine as "a pestilential error."[7] The doctrine is rejected by the most significant Reformed confessions, including the Westminster Confession of Faith (29.2).

It is clear, then, that there is a significant point of difference between the Roman Catholic doctrine of the Lord's Supper and the Protestant doctrine on this point. But why did the Protestant Reformers reject the doctrine of the sacrifice of the Mass? First, and most importantly, this doctrine was rejected because it was seen to be in direct contradiction with the Word of God. According to Scripture, Jesus is our Great High Priest (Heb. 4:14; 5:5, 10; 6:20). He is contrasted with the priests of the old covenant. Under the old covenant, there were many priests because death prevented any one priest from remaining in office, but Christ remains a priest forever (7:23–24). Also, under the old covenant, the priests offered sacrifices daily for their own sins and the sins of others, but Christ has no need to do so (7:27). Christ offered Himself, not repeatedly, but once and for all (9:25–28).

This is the key point, and it is one that the book of Hebrews emphasizes over and over again. Jesus' sacrifice was a once-for-all offering that has been completed. It is a finished work. The author of Hebrews emphasizes the point, saying: "And every priest stands daily at his service, offering repeatedly the same sacrifices, which can never take away sins. But when Christ had offered for all time a single sacrifice for sins, he sat down at the right hand of God, waiting from that time until his enemies should be made a footstool for his feet. For by a single offering he has perfected for all time those who are being sanctified" (10:11–14). In other words, Christ's sacrifice is a completed act. "We have been sanctified through the offering of the body of Jesus Christ once for all" (v. 10). The Lord's Supper is nowhere described in a way that suggests any contradiction with this point. It is not described as a re-presentation or a continuation of Christ's completed sacrifice. It is certainly not described as a propitiatory sacrifice.

In the writings of the early church, we do find some of the fathers using the language of "sacrifice" in reference to the Lord's Supper. Some associate it with the offering mentioned in Malachi 1:11. Others refer to it as a sacrifice of praise and thanks or an offering of the bread and wine to God as an act of thanksgiving. This is most likely the reason why the Lord's Supper began to be spoken of as the "Eucharist" (Greek for "thanksgiving") from a very early point in time. Cyprian of Carthage, in the third century, appears to be the first Christian writer to speak of the supper as a sacrifice of Christ Himself.[8]

As we have already seen, the best way to understand the connection between the once-and-for-all completed sacrifice of Christ and the Lord's Supper is to understand the supper as something akin to an Old Testament sacrificial meal.[9] This element of the Old Testament sacrificial law is seen in the description of the peace offering in Leviticus 3 and 7 and in the Passover. The regulations concerning several of the Levitical offerings allowed the priests to eat a portion of the sacrifice. Only the peace offering, however, allowed the Israelite people to partake. The Passover sacrifice as well allowed the people to partake of the slain sacrificial lamb in the Passover meal.

The key point to keep in mind with both the Passover and the Levitical peace offering is that, in both, the *act of offering* the sacrifice is distinct from the *eating* of the sacrificed animal. This is most clearly seen in the law concerning the peace offering because the act of sacrifice could be done only by a legitimately ordained priest. The Israelites who were not priests did not participate in this act of offering the sacrifice, but they did partake in the act of eating the already sacrificed animal. These are two distinct actions.

Similarly, Christ our High Priest is the only one who could legitimately offer Himself in the once-for-all act of sacrifice that the Old Testament rites foreshadowed. He was both the High Priest who offered the sacrifice and the sacrificial Lamb itself. Uniquely, in the history of redemption, Jesus Christ was both Priest and Lamb. Because of the sacramental union between the sign and the thing signified, when Christians partake of the bread and wine, they partake of the body and blood of Christ in the manner explained above. They partake of the Lamb who was *already* sacrificed once and for all. They do not participate in the *already completed* once-for-all self-offering of Christ, which only He as the Great High Priest could legitimately accomplish. The offering of the sacrificial Lamb and the eating of the already offered sacrificial Lamb are two different acts.

CHAPTER 8

WHAT ARE THE ELEMENTS
OF THE LORD'S SUPPER?

The elements used by Christ in the institution of the Lord's
Supper were bread and wine, and the elements used
throughout the history of the church have been bread and
wine. There would be little more to say about this question had
controversies not arisen in the church regarding both of these
elements. In the early church, for example, debates arose regarding whether leavened or unleavened bread should be used. In
the nineteenth century, the anti-alcohol Temperance Movement led many Christians to replace wine with grape juice. In
recent decades, some Christians have begun using things such
as cola and corn chips. But does it really matter what elements
we use? Most Christians believe, for good reasons, that it does
matter.

Jesus, on the night He was betrayed, during the Jewish
Passover, took bread and, after giving thanks, broke it and said:
"This is my body, which is for you. Do this in remembrance

of me." Then after supper, He took the cup and said: "This cup is the new covenant in my blood. Do this, as often as you drink it, in remembrance of me" (1 Cor. 11:23–25). In the Synoptic Gospels, Jesus identifies the contents of the cup as the "fruit of the vine" (Matt. 26:29; Mark 14:25; Luke 22:18). In this context, the phrase "the fruit of the vine" means "wine."[1] When Jesus says, "Do this," part of what is entailed is the partaking of the bread and wine. We are not authorized to use anything other than these elements any more than Old Testament Israelites were authorized to change the elements of the Passover.

If we agree on this point, does it settle all of the questions? Unfortunately, no. Other questions immediately arise. Regarding the bread, should it be a single loaf or pre-divided pieces? Should the bread be leavened or unleavened? Although the Bible does not explicitly address the first question, there are hints that the supper as practiced in the New Testament involved the use of a single loaf. The supper is described in the book of Acts in terms of "breaking" bread (2:42). Paul also describes it as "the bread that we break" in 1 Corinthians 10:16. Although this language is not clear enough to be dogmatic, the language does make more sense if the supper as observed in the New Testament involved a single loaf.

The question regarding the use of leavened or unleavened bread is more difficult to answer. Most Protestants have deemed the question a nonessential matter. For other churches it has been a much more significant issue. It became a point of disagreement in the Middle Ages. The church in the East used leavened bread, while the Latin Church in the West used unleavened bread. Each side had its arguments, but many of these were based on local church customs. It was difficult to make an argument based on a clear command of Scripture.

We know that the Lord's Supper was instituted at the Jewish Passover, which entailed the use of unleavened bread. On the other hand, the word used for "bread" in connection with the Lord's Supper is *artos* rather than *azymos*. While *azymos* is the Greek word used for unleavened bread, the word *artos* refers to ordinary bread.[2] It has been suggested that Jesus used unleavened bread because that was the only kind of bread available at a Passover meal, but this suggestion seems to sever the link between the Passover and the Lord's Supper, making the Passover setting of negligible importance. The link between the Passover and the Lord's Supper is important, but the practice of the Lord's Supper as described in the book of Acts does not appear to require either leavened or unleavened bread.

What about the use of wine? This was not a question or debate in any part of the church for the first 1,800 years of its existence. The use of wine (sometimes mixed with water) was the universal practice of the church until the nineteenth century when some churches (particularly in the United States) concluded that the use of alcohol is inherently sinful and thus replaced wine with grape juice. Since the nineteenth century, many Protestant churches have followed this line of thinking, and the use of grape juice as an element in the Lord's Supper is now seen by many as the norm. The case can be made that the replacement of wine with grape juice was not justifiable on biblical grounds and that wine is the element Jesus Christ intended the church to use in the celebration of the Lord's Supper.

Because the main objection to the use of wine is that all alcoholic beverages are inherently sinful, we must turn to the Scripture to see that this is not the case. The Bible everywhere condemns the abuse of alcohol and drunkenness, but it nowhere states or implies that alcoholic beverages in and of themselves are sinful. Instead, the Scriptures declare wine to be a good gift from God to be enjoyed in moderation. A further proof of this biblical doctrine is the fact that Jesus Christ Himself, God incarnate, made wine and drank wine. Since He was without sin, it simply cannot be argued that the use of wine is inherently sinful.

When we look at the Old Testament, we see that God Himself commands that wine be brought as an offering to Himself (Ex. 29: 40; Lev. 23:13; Num. 15:5, 7, 10; 28:7). God never commands that something unclean or unholy be offered to Himself, yet He commands that wine be offered. The implication is that wine is something good. We also see in Scripture that wine is described as a blessing from God (Gen. 27:28; Deut. 7:12–13; 11:13–14; 14:22–26; Judg. 9:13; Ps. 104:14–15; Prov. 3:9–10; Amos 9:13–14). If alcoholic beverages were inherently sinful, the giving of wine would be described as a curse, not a blessing. What is instead described as a curse is the *removal* of wine (Deut. 28:15, 39; Isa. 62:8). Furthermore, wine was enjoyed at David's coronation banquet (1 Chron. 12:38–40), and it is used as a symbol of the gospel (Isa. 55:1).

It is to be part of the great eschatological feast *prepared by the Lord Himself* (Isa. 25:6). When God Himself prepares a meal that includes wine, we are on seriously dangerous ground when we claim that wine is evil. Obviously, the abuse of wine is described as sinful (e.g., Prov. 20:1; 23:20–21; Isa. 5:11, 22; 28:7–8), but the sin of drunkenness no more means that wine is inherently evil than the sin of gluttony means that food is inherently evil.

When we turn to the New Testament, we see that Jesus Himself drank wine. Jesus said to the crowds: "For John the Baptist has come eating no bread and drinking no wine, and you say, 'He has a demon.' The Son of Man has come eating and drinking, and you say, 'Look at him! A glutton and a drunkard, a friend of tax collectors and sinners!'" (Luke 7:33–34). John was condemned by the Jews for not eating bread and not drinking wine. Jesus was condemned for eating bread and drinking wine. They even called Him a drunkard, something they would not have done had He drunk only unfermented grape juice.

Not only did Jesus Himself drink wine, He made wine for the guests at a party (John 2:1–11). The word used in this passage is *oinos*, which means fermented wine.[3] It is not used in the Bible to refer to unfermented grape juice. When we see how the Bible itself speaks of wine, we can understand why it is no scandal for Jesus to have drunk wine and made wine. We can also understand why it is not a problem to acknowledge that Jesus instituted the Lord's Supper with real fermented wine. God's good gifts are not evil. It is only the abuse of those gifts that is sinful.

It is also worth reminding ourselves that the use of wine was never an issue in the entire history of the church until the nineteenth century. It was the universally accepted practice regardless of denomination. Wine was universally used in the early church, East and West, although it was often mixed with water. At the time of the Protestant Reformation, the Lutherans, Anglicans, and Anabaptists all used wine in the supper.[4] The Reformed churches also understood wine to be the biblically mandated element to be used in the supper.[5] The Baptist churches confessed the same regarding the use of wine.[6] There was no significant dissent on this issue.

Despite the clear biblical and historical testimony to Jesus' use of wine in the institution of the Lord's Supper, some today object. As we have seen, the most significant objection is that any use of alcoholic beverages is sinful. This objection has already been addressed and shown to be contrary to biblical teaching, but are there other objections? Yes. The most popular objection is that we should not use wine because some people are born with a genetic predisposition toward alcoholism, and the use of wine could potentially lead them to become alcoholics.

The first and most important point that has to be taken into consideration when thinking about this objection is that God knows the sins to which people are prone, and yet God instituted the Lord's Supper with wine anyway. If He is all-wise, and He is, then we have to follow His wisdom and not our own on this point. A second point that must be remembered is that drunkenness is a sin, a moral failure. It cannot be explained away simply as a "disease," a term often used to avoid personal responsibility for moral failure. Third, we must remember that human nature has not changed in two thousand years. If the use of a small amount of alcohol can cause people to become alcoholics today and that is a good reason to not use wine, the same was true two thousand years ago, and if this was true two thousand years ago, Jesus was potentially guilty of gross negligence at best when He made wine and instituted the Lord's Supper with wine. Finally, throughout church history, the wine has often been mixed with water. This drastically reduces the already miniscule amount of alcohol contained in a single sip of wine.

CHAPTER 9

HOW FREQUENTLY SHOULD THE LORD'S SUPPER BE OBSERVED?

C hurches in the Reformed tradition have come to different conclusions regarding how often the Lord's Supper should be observed. Some Reformed churches observe the sacrament every Lord's Day. Others, probably the majority, observe it monthly. Some observe it every other month, and some observe it quarterly. There are likely some that observe the supper annually. The decision has usually been left to the discretion of the elders of each local church. The main reason for this variety in practice is the fact that there is not an explicit command in the New Testament regarding how often the supper should be observed. What direction we find is implicit.

When we examine the book of Acts, for example, it appears that the observance of the Lord's Supper was a part of the regular worship. After Peter's Pentecost sermon, many Israelites repented, and about three thousand were saved (Acts 2:41).

We then see what these new believers did: "And they devoted themselves to the apostles' teaching and the fellowship, to the breaking of bread and the prayers" (Acts 2:42). If "the breaking of bread" is a reference to the Lord's Supper, then the supper was as much a part of the regular gathering as the Apostles' teaching and prayer.

The argument has been made that "the breaking of bread" refers simply to a regular meal. In some contexts, this may be the case, but in the context of Acts, it seems unlikely. Acts 20:7, for example, refers to "the first day of the week, when we gathered together to break bread." If "the breaking of bread" refers to their regular meals, the implication of Acts 20:7 would be that they ate a regular meal only once a week. There is no indication elsewhere in the New Testament that Christians ate food only once a week. It seems clear that what Luke is speaking of here is the sacrament of the Lord's Supper, which was observed on the first day of each week.

The earliest Christian writings after the New Testament point to the continuation of the practice of a weekly observance of the Lord's Supper. The *Didache* (c. 50–150) speaks of gathering on the Lord's Day to break bread and give thanks (14.1). Again, the reference to the breaking of bread in this context most likely refers to the Lord's Supper. The early apologist Justin Martyr (c. 100–165) provides a detailed description of the church's weekly worship service in his *First Apology* (section 67). In it, he describes Christians gathering on Sunday. He notes that the writings of the Apostles and prophets are read for as long as time permits. This is followed by prayer. Finally, the

Lord's Supper is observed. All of these things are described as regular elements of the weekly worship of the church.

For a variety of reasons, throughout the Middle Ages, the Lord's Supper, or Eucharist, began to be observed less and less frequently by the laity. In 1215, the Fourth Lateran Council mandated that believers partake of the sacrament at least once a year. This is significant because many evangelical Protestants object to a frequent observance of the Lord's Supper, thinking that it is a Roman Catholic practice. In fact, the opposite is the case. Every indication is that the New Testament church and the early post-Apostolic church observed the supper at least weekly, and that infrequent communion was a later development in the practice of the medieval Roman Catholic Church.

The great second-generation Reformer John Calvin objected to this practice of the late-medieval church. He rejected infrequent communion and argued that the church should return to the practice of the first centuries. Calvin writes, "Plainly this custom which enjoins us to take communion once a year is a veritable invention of the devil, whoever was instrumental in introducing it" (*Institutes*, 4.17.46). He continues: "It should have been done far differently: the Lord's Table should have been spread at least once a week for the assembly of Christians, and the promises declared in it should feed us spiritually. None is indeed to be forcibly compelled, but all are to be urged and aroused; also the inertia of indolent people is to be rebuked. All, like hungry men, should flock to such a bounteous repast" (4.17.46). Frequent (at least weekly) observance of the Lord's Supper is not, then, a Roman Catholic practice. It is what

Reformers such as Calvin urged to oppose the Roman Catholic practice of infrequent communion.

Calvin was unable to convince the city of Geneva to adopt weekly observance of the Lord's Supper. The city council instead pushed for quarterly communion. Calvin went along with this, but he was clearly not pleased. He wrote in regard to this situation, "I have taken care to record publicly that our custom is defective, so that those who come after me may be able to correct it the more freely and easily."[1] In other words, he went along with the city council of Geneva hoping that those who came after him would be able to move the church to a weekly observance of the Lord's Supper. It is evident that those who came after Calvin have yet to be able to "correct" the practice, because the majority of Reformed churches have never observed the Lord's Supper as frequently as Calvin desired. It was ultimately left to the discretion of each local church. As the Westminster Directory for the Public Worship of God put it: "The communion, or supper of the Lord, is frequently to be celebrated; but how often, may be considered and determined by the ministers, and other church-governors of each congregation, as they shall find most convenient for the comfort and edification of the people committed to their charge."

What were the reasons behind Calvin's goal? Why was he so desirous of *at least* weekly observance of the supper? It was because of his understanding of the nature of the sacrament. Those with a different understanding of the nature of the sacrament will have a different understanding regarding its observance. As indicated above, there are different views regarding the nature of the

Lord's Supper within the Reformed churches. If one holds to a view similar to that of Zwingli, which sees the supper largely as a matter of subjective mental recollection, it will be difficult to understand any need for frequent observance. If the whole point of the sacrament is merely to think about what Jesus did on the cross, well, we can do that anywhere at any time. However, if one holds to a view that understands the supper to be a real means of grace given to us by our Savior, then arguments for more frequent observance begin to make sense.

Consider again what the Westminster Confession of Faith says regarding the nature of the Lord's Supper. It tells us that our Lord instituted this sacrament for us "for the perpetual remembrance of the sacrifice of Himself in His death; the sealing all benefits thereof unto true believers, their spiritual nourishment and growth in Him, their further engagement in and to all duties which they owe unto Him; and to be a bond and pledge of their communion with Him, and with each other, as members of His mystical body" (29.1). It continues, "Worthy receivers outwardly partaking of the visible elements in this sacrament, do then also, inwardly by faith, really and indeed, yet not carnally and corporally, but spiritually, receive and feed upon Christ crucified, and all benefits of His death" (29.7). Do we really believe this about the supper? If so, the very way we approach the question of frequency changes. Why would we *not* want to receive as often as possible these gracious benefits offered to us by the Lord? Why would we want to observe a fast regarding a meal provided specifically for our spiritual nourishment?

The most often cited reason for not observing the Lord's Supper every time the church gathers for worship is that there is no explicit command to do so in the New Testament. Given this fact, it is argued, local churches are free to celebrate the supper as frequently or as infrequently as they wish. Granted, there is no explicit command to observe the supper every time the church gathers, but it should be kept in mind that there is also no explicit command to do all of the other things we do in worship every time we gather. There is no explicit command to preach weekly, teach weekly, pray weekly, or sing weekly. We do all of these things every time we gather because of the example of the early church described in passages such as Acts 2:42. But that passage, it must be remembered, also includes the Lord's Supper.

Another objection heard in some Reformed circles is that frequent observance of the supper is a Roman Catholic practice. We have already seen that this idea is historically mistaken. It simply is not true. Protestant Reformers such as John Calvin argued *for* frequent (at least weekly) communion, not against it. If an argument for weekly observance of the supper is inherently Roman Catholic, then we are in the awkward position of having to say that Calvin himself was advocating this view. It is also worth mentioning at this point that the mere fact that the Roman Catholic Church believes or practices something does not automatically render it unbiblical. The Roman Catholic Church believes in the Trinity and the incarnation and the bodily resurrection of Christ. So do we. The Roman Catholic Church reads Scripture during its gatherings for worship. So do we. The Protestant Reformers were just that—*Reformers*. Their goal was to correct abuses in doctrine and practice, not to throw the baby out with the bathwater.

Some have objected that frequent communion would obscure the centrality of the preaching of the Word. For that to happen, however, there would have to be a serious misunderstanding of both the preached Word and the sacrament. Can that happen? Of course, and the Reformers had seen it happen. Yet this did not cause them to advocate less frequent observance of the supper. It caused them to advocate a correct understanding of the relationship between the preaching of the Word and the observance of the supper. They argued that the sacrament is a seal of the covenant of grace, a seal of the promises of the gospel. They argued that it is complementary to the preaching of the Word.

A final objection that is sometimes mentioned is that frequent observation of the Lord's Supper would make it less meaningful and significant. If Christians were to observe the supper weekly, it is suggested, the sacrament would not be as special. Two points might be offered in response to this objection. First, the Lord's Supper is a God-ordained means of grace. It is something that the Lord Himself has provided for our spiritual nourishment, just as He has provided the preaching of the Word. We do not say that we should sit under the ministry of the Word less frequently lest familiarity breed contempt. We do not say that we should pray less frequently lest prayer become less meaningful and significant. Can familiarity with preaching and prayer breed contempt? Of course. But that does not mean that we should do these things less often. Nor should we observe the supper less often simply because there is a possibility that we fail to treat this sacrament as it should be treated.

Second, the Lord's Supper becomes less meaningful and significant only when we fail to truly understand its meaning and significance. Again, our understanding of the nature of this sacrament is often very much connected with our understanding of how frequently it should be observed. The only way we can understand why Calvin, for example, believed that the supper should be observed *at least* weekly is to understand what he believed about the nature of the Lord's Supper. We live in a generation that is spiritually starving. The Westminster Confession teaches that the Lord's Supper is provided by the Lord for our spiritual nourishment. It is not the only thing God has provided, of course, and it cannot be separated from the Word, but perhaps we should seriously consider whether there is a connection between our less frequent use of this God-ordained means of spiritual nourishment and the decline in our spiritual health.

CHAPTER 10

HOW SHOULD BELIEVERS PREPARE FOR AND PARTAKE OF THE LORD'S SUPPER?

Whether our church observes the Lord's Supper weekly, monthly, or quarterly, how should we as Christians prepare for the observance of this sacrament when we do observe it, and how should we receive it? These are important questions. It is not enough merely to have a right understanding of the definition of and nature of the supper. We must also take seriously the manner in which we partake of this sacrament. Paul tell us in 1 Corinthians 11:27, "Whoever, therefore, eats the bread or drinks the cup of the Lord in an unworthy manner will be guilty concerning the body and blood of the Lord." The manner, therefore, in which we observe the sacrament must be taken seriously.

It is important to consider this question, because many

Christians are partaking of the Lord's Supper without any thought whatsoever. They may not understand the holy nature of the sacrament because they have not been instructed properly. There may be other reasons. Regardless of the reasons, too many believers come to the table without having given any thought to what they are doing and why they are doing it. During the observance of the sacrament, they allow their minds to wander, thinking about the football game on television that afternoon or the movie they watched the night before. As the elements are distributed, they may get impatient, wondering, "How long is this going to take?" Such thoughts betray an unbiblical attitude toward the sacrament that Christ instituted for the benefit of His people. It is necessary, therefore, to consider how we are to approach the table of the Lord.

The most helpful instructions for those preparing to observe the Lord's Supper are found in the Westminster Larger Catechism, questions 171–75. This catechism is very practical and pastoral in its approach to these issues, and an examination of its words will prove instructive. The first question asked regarding preparation is this:

How are they that receive the sacrament of the Lord's Supper to prepare themselves before they come unto it? They that receive the sacrament of the Lord's Supper are, before they come, to prepare themselves thereunto, by examining themselves of their being in Christ, of their sins and wants; of the truth and measure of their knowledge, faith, repentance; love to God and the brethren, charity to all men, forgiving those that have done them wrong; of their desires after Christ, and of their new obedience; and by renewing the exercise of these graces, by serious meditation, and fervent prayer. (WLC 171)

In short, Christians are to prepare themselves for the Lord's Supper through honest and prayerful self-examination. Because the supper is a means of spiritual nourishment, the catechism is urging believers to be aware of their spiritual state and spiritual needs.

In question 172, the catechism asks whether those who have doubts regarding their faith or their preparation may come to the table. The answer helpfully recognizes that all Christians have doubts and that no Christian is always going to be perfectly prepared. However, if such Christians realize that they lack full assurance and if they desire "to be found in Christ and to depart from iniquity," they ought to come to the supper in order to be strengthened. Significantly, the catechism emphasizes that the Lord's Supper is "for the relief even of weak and doubting Christians." Only those who "are found to be ignorant or scandalous" are to be kept from the supper until such time as they might "receive instruction and manifest their reformation" (WLC 173). In short, the Lord's Supper is not for Christians who have reached perfect sinlessness in this life. They don't exist. It is for repentant and repenting Christians.

The catechism continues by providing helpful instruction

for believers regarding what they are to do at the time the supper is being administered.

> It is required of them that receive the sacrament of the Lord's Supper, that, during the time of the administration of it, with all holy reverence and attention they wait upon God in that ordinance, diligently observe the sacramental elements and actions, heedfully discern the Lord's body, and affectionately meditate on his death and sufferings, and thereby stir up themselves to a vigorous exercise of their graces; in judging themselves, and sorrowing for sin; in earnest hungering and thirsting after Christ, feeding on him by faith, receiving of his fulness, trusting in his merits, rejoicing in his love, giving thanks for his grace; in renewing of their covenant with God, and love to all the saints. (WLC 174)

Several distinct instructions are provided here. We are to reverently wait on God. Acknowledging that He is infinitely sovereign and holy, we do not presume on His grace. We must recognize that we are standing on holy ground and must treat the observance of this sacrament accordingly.

Furthermore, we are to diligently observe the sacramental elements and actions. Given that they are signs, we must understand the reality that they signify. We are thus to "discern the Lord's body," understanding the nature of the bread as a sign of the body of Christ and the nature of the wine as a sign of the new covenant in His blood. We are to understand that these signs are in a sacramental union with the realities they signify. The catechism continues, explaining that we are to meditate on Christ's death and sufferings, recognizing that He suffered and died for us while we were still enemies. Those who do meditate on His death and sufferings will have a truly godly sorrow for their sins and a truly grateful heart for the forgiveness obtained through the shedding of His blood.

The catechism explains that we are to hunger and thirst after Christ, feeding on Him by faith. In other words, we are to desire communion with Him and faithfully feed on Him with the means provided by the Lord Himself. The psalmist describes a soul that pants for and thirsts for God in Psalm 42:1–2. This ought to describe our desire for communion with Christ. We will not desire Christ in this way until and unless we truly grasp our need for Him, our need for His grace and His mercy. We are also to understand that when we partake of the supper in faith, we truly partake of Christ. Again, this requires a proper understanding of the nature of this sacrament and the relationship between the sacramental signs and the realities they signify.

We are to trust in His merits, understanding that we are justified on the grounds of His imputed righteousness. We are to rejoice in His love for us, a love that is infinite and perfect, a love that will never cease. We are to give thanks for His grace toward us, understanding that what we deserved was His wrath. The catechism continues by saying that we are to renew our covenant with God. Our covenant with God is the covenant of grace; thus, to renew it is to renew our commitment to depend on His grace for our needs. We are to renew our commitment to follow Christ in dependence on His grace to stand. Finally, we are to show love to all the saints. Our communion with Christ involves our communion with the saints, and we cannot desire or love Christ without a corresponding desire for communion with and love for His people, our brothers and sisters.

This section of the catechism closes with the question, "What is the duty of Christians, after they have received the sacrament of the Lord's Supper?" Answer:

The duty of Christians, after they have received the sacrament of the Lord's Supper, is seriously to consider: How they have behaved themselves therein, and with: What success; if they find quickening and comfort, to bless God for it, beg the continuance of it, watch against relapses, fulfil their vows, and encourage themselves to a frequent attendance on that ordinance: but if they find no present benefit, more exactly to review their preparation to, and carriage at, the sacrament; in both which, if they can approve themselves to God and their own consciences, they are to wait for the fruit of it in due time: but, if they see they have failed in either, they are to be humbled, and to attend upon it afterwards with more care and diligence. (WLC 175)

Just as self-examination is to precede the observance of the supper, self-examination is to follow it.

Believers are instructed here to seriously consider whether we observed the sacrament accordingly and whether we were strengthened and comforted in and by this means of grace. If so, the catechism reminds us that we are to thank God for such grace, beg that He continue to give us this grace, beware of relapses into sinful behavior, fulfill any vows we have made, and be encouraged to partake of the sacrament frequently. If we have not been strengthened and encouraged in the observance of the sacrament, we are to seek to understand the reasons why. The catechism recommends considering how we prepared for the partaking of the supper and how we actually partook of it. If we have prepared for and have partaken of the sacrament faithfully, then we are to wait on God, trusting that He has a good reason for making us endure such a trial. If we recognize that we have sinned or been lax in our preparation or in our partaking, this should drive us to repent and humbly seek, by God's grace, to avoid such sins in the future.

There are some who believe that the kind of self-examination prescribed in the catechism leads to morbid introspection. Obviously, this can be the result if we have a distorted and unbiblical view of justification and/or sanctification, but if we know what the Scripture teaches regarding justification and sanctification, we have no need to play down those texts of Scripture that encourage self-examination. Paul clearly states in 1 Corinthians 11:28, "Let a person *examine himself*, then, and so eat of the bread and drink of the cup" (emphasis added). This is the Word of God telling us to examine ourselves. We see something similar in 2 Corinthians 13:5. There,

Paul writes: "*Examine yourselves*, to see whether you are in the faith. *Test yourselves*" (emphases added). We are justified by faith alone in Christ alone, but true faith bears fruit. The kind of self-examination encouraged by Scripture and by the catechism in connection with the Lord's Supper is one that is honestly seeking to determine whether there is any such fruit of the Spirit. Let us dedicate ourselves anew to preparing for and partaking of the Lord's Supper with a heart focused on our Lord Jesus Christ.

CHAPTER 11

SHOULD CHILDREN PARTAKE OF THE LORD'S SUPPER?

When my son was very young, perhaps four or five years old, he was sitting with our family as the Lord's Supper was observed in our local church. The bread and wine were distributed, but since he was not yet a communicant member, he did not receive the elements. He asked me why he could not eat and drink, and protested, "But I love Jesus too!" This is a situation many Christian parents have faced. But how do we respond? Should children partake of the Lord's Supper? If so, at what age? These questions have been the source of some controversy within Reformed churches, and the debate over what is termed *paedocommunion* continues.[1]

There is no clear evidence regarding whether children participated in the supper during the first two centuries of the church. The evidence becomes somewhat clearer in the following centuries. What evidence we have indicates that in the

Western church between the third and twelfth centuries, it was not uncommon for children to partake of the supper. Children of believers continue to this day to be admitted to the sacrament in the Eastern Orthodox Church. The practice gradually fell out of favor in the Western church. It has been argued that as the doctrine of transubstantiation became more and more ingrained in the mind of the church, the fear arose that children would spill the blood or drop the body of Christ.

Most of the Protestant Reformers opposed the practice of admitting young children to the Lord's Supper, but not because of the doctrine of transubstantiation, which they rejected. They opposed allowing children to partake because they believed that only those who are able to examine themselves are allowed to partake of the sacrament. John Calvin granted that the early church allowed young children to partake, but he argued that this practice had "deservedly fallen into disuse" (*Institutes*, 4.16.30). The Westminster Standards followed Calvin on this point. Question 177 of the Westminster Larger Catechism is clear, saying that the Lord's Supper is to be administered "only to such as are of years and ability to examine themselves."

The question became a serious point of debate again in Reformed churches in the 1970s when several articles by Reformed theologians were published advocating paedocommunion. Since that time, numerous books and articles have been written on all sides of the debate. On one side, there are those who argue for the common Reformed practice that admits baptized Christians to the table sometime during adolescence when they are clearly able to examine themselves. This view is now sometimes termed *credocommunion*. Among those who argue that younger children should be admitted to the table, at least two different positions exist. Some argue that all baptized members of the church, including infants and young children, are entitled to receive the Lord's Supper. This view has been termed "strict" paedocommunion or covenant communion.[2] Others argue that younger children can be admitted when they make an age-appropriate confession of faith. This has been termed "soft" paedocommunion.[3]

It is not possible in this short space to get into all of the intricacies of this debate. Suffice it to say that the most important passage of Scripture to consider in connection with this question is 1 Corinthians 11:17–34. In this passage, Paul provides us with his most general instructions for the observance of the supper, and he makes several points that are relevant to the debate. First, he reminds the Corinthians that Jesus said, regarding both the eating of the bread and the drinking of the wine, "Do this in remembrance of me" (vv. 24–25). Why is this relevant to the paedocommunion debate? Because remembrance requires a certain level of cognitive maturity not discernible in infants.

Second, and even more importantly, Paul gives explicit instructions regarding what Christians are to do before partaking of the supper. He writes in verse 28: "Let a person examine himself, then, and so eat of the bread and drink of the cup." He then adds in verse 29, "For anyone who eats and drinks without discerning the body eats and drinks judgment on himself." Those who partake of the Lord's Supper, then, are required to examine themselves and to discern the body of Christ. Both of these require a certain level of cognitive ability, and the first, at least, requires self-awareness. What is clearly required is the ability to recognize the existence of one's own faith and repentance.

The biblical requirements for partaking of the Lord's Supper found in 1 Corinthians 11 rule out the "strong" paedocommunion view. These requirements rule out the possibility of administering the bread and wine to infants and small toddlers who do not have the cognitive maturity and ability to do these things in remembrance of Christ, to examine themselves, and to discern the body of Christ. Such requires the ability to be taught what these things mean. It requires having some grasp of the meaning of sin, and faith, and redemption. To partake of the supper without self-examination is to invite the judgment of God (vv. 27–29).

When considering those permitted by Scripture to partake of the Lord's Supper, we are looking at those who have the cognitive maturity and ability to recognize their own sin and their need of the Savior. We are looking, in other words, at those who have the cognitive ability to make a coherent and credible profession of faith. The question, then, is whether this also rules out the so-called "soft" paedocommunion view. Recall that according to this view, younger children can be admitted to the table when they make an age-appropriate confession of faith. Is this view consistent with Scripture, or should we have all children wait until adolescence before they are admitted to the supper?

There is obviously wisdom in waiting, and churches that choose this option should not be condemned. Children do not develop cognitively at the same rate. Thus, an argument can be made that it is best to wait until an age when almost all children have developed the ability for self-examination. It saves the elders from the difficult task of having to discern the cognitive development of each child on a case-by-case basis. Proponents might also urge that given the danger of inviting the judgment of God, this is the safest course of action for all involved—the elders responsible for admitting communicant members and the children of believing church members.

On the other hand, the fact that children do not cognitively develop at the same rate could be a good reason for allowing age-appropriate professions of faith. In fact, because this view requires a profession of faith, it is probably best not to refer to it as paedocommunion at all. Such terminology only confuses the issue because there is a vast difference between those who argue that all baptized members of the church, including infants and young children, are entitled to receive the Lord's Supper and those who argue that while a profession of faith is required, a set age requirement is somewhat arbitrary. The term *paedocommunion* should be reserved for those who believe that baptism is the one requirement for receiving the Lord's Supper.

Arguably, the two remaining views are both consistent with the biblical requirements for self-examination and a profession of faith. In favor of the view requiring merely an age-appropriate profession of faith, it is important to note that not only do children cognitively develop at different rates, adults themselves are at different levels of cognitive ability. Some adults never develop a cognitive ability higher than that of a child, and some adults have highly developed cognitive abilities. There is an enormous range of cognitive abilities even among physically mature adults. This must be taken into account when considering this question.

Furthermore, some adults, due to age, injury, or disease, see their fully developed cognitive abilities decrease significantly. Some adults reach the point where their cognitive abilities are not much different from that of a young child. If a child of seven or eight is not allowed to partake of the supper because of having cognitive abilities that are less than those of a normally developed mature adult, consistency would seem to require that we not allow adults to partake if they never reach that stage of development or if they mentally regress to that stage due to age, injury, or disease. This too must be taken into consideration. In other words, if cognitive ability is going to be the most significant determining factor, then we are not merely talking about young children.

It might be better to speak not only of an age-appropriate profession of faith but of a profession of faith appropriate to whatever one's cognitive ability is. If we recognize that there is a range of cognitive abilities and levels of development among children *and* adults and that some children are more cognitively developed than some adults, we can consider this question more carefully and objectively. Arbitrary age limits do not seem to take all of this into consideration. If a church does choose to allow for professions of faith appropriate to an individual's cognitive ability, elders will have to take the time to deal with each member on a case-by-case basis. This means that a particular five-year-old in the church may be ready to partake of the Lord's Supper in a biblically appropriate manner while a particular twelve-year-old is not. For that matter, it may be the case that one thirty-year-old is ready while another thirty-year-old is not.

Requiring a profession of faith appropriate to one's cognitive ability for both children and adults does not leave infants and toddlers outside of the church family any more than giving a baby or toddler a bottle of milk at Thanksgiving while the rest of the family has turkey and dressing leaves that baby or toddler out. Some activities and responsibilities in the church have requirements that not every member can fulfill. We don't ordain three-year-olds to the ministry of the Word, but they are still part of the church. The church is a body, and different members of the body have different functions. A kidney cannot fulfill the requirements necessary to be the heart or the lungs. This doesn't mean that the kidney is not a necessary and important part of the body. It simply means that it isn't the heart or lungs. Just as we do not admit someone to the pulpit who cannot read, we do not admit someone to the table who cannot examine himself.

When my son asked me why he couldn't eat the bread and wine, it gave me the opportunity to talk to him about the meaning of the sacrament. I explained to him that God has certain requirements for participation, and that if he met those requirements he could talk to our elders, and they would determine whether he was to be admitted as a communicant member. He was no longer confused. Instead, he was encouraged by this information and began to study at a level appropriate to his age. The elders later examined him. He made an age-appropriate confession of faith and was admitted to the table as a communicant member of the church.

NOTES

Chapter 1

1 A good introduction to all of these doctrines is the Westminster Confession of Faith and Catechisms. The reader is encouraged to review these confessional documents in order to gain a better grasp of the doctrinal context for a proper understanding of the Lord's Supper.

Chapter 2

1 For a helpful introduction to the various views, see John H. Armstrong, ed., *Understanding Four Views on the Lord's Supper* (Grand Rapids, Mich.: Zondervan, 2007); Gordon T. Smith, ed., *The Lord's Supper: Five Views* (Downers Grove, Ill.: IVP Academic, 2008).

2 For a contemporary conservative restatement of the Lutheran doctrine, see John R. Stephenson, *The Lord's Supper* (St. Louis: The Luther Academy, 2003).

3 For a concise statement of Zwingli's doctrine, see W.P. Stephens, *The Theology of Huldrych Zwingli* (Oxford, England: Clarendon, 1986), 218–59.

4 A classic study of Calvin's doctrine of the Lord's Supper is B.A. Gerrish, *Grace and Gratitude: The Eucharistic Theology of John Calvin* (Eugene, Ore.: Wipf and Stock, 2002).

5 For a more complete discussion of the views of Luther, Zwingli, and Calvin, see my chapter in Matthew Barrett, ed., *Reformation Theology: A Systematic Summary* (Wheaton, Ill.: Crossway, 2017), 643–74.

6 See my *Given For You: Reclaiming Calvin's Doctrine of the Lord's Supper* (Phillipsburg, N.J.: P&R, 2002).

7 For a contemporary statement of the Baptist doctrine, see Thomas R. Schreiner and Matthew R. Crawford, *The Lord's Supper* (Nashville, Tenn.: Broadman & Holman, 2010).

NOTES

Chapter 3

1 The exodus motif is a key theme throughout Scripture. See Bryan D. Estelle, *Echoes of Exodus: Tracing a Biblical Motif* (Downers Grove, Ill.: IVP Academic, 2018); see also Alastair J. Roberts and Andrew Wilson, *Echoes of Exodus: Tracing Themes of Redemption through Scripture* (Wheaton, Ill.: Crossway, 2018).
2 See David E. Holwerda, *Jesus and Israel: One Covenant or Two?* (Grand Rapids, Mich.: Eerdmans, 1995).

Chapter 5

1 Benjamin B. Warfield, "The Fundamental Significance of the Lord's Supper," in *Selected Shorter Writings of Benjamin B. Warfield*, ed. John E. Meeter (Phillipsburg, N.J.: P&R, 1970), I.332–38.
2 Warfield, "Fundamental Significance," I.336–37; cf. also L. Michael Morales, *Who Shall Ascend the Mountain of the Lord? A Biblical Theology of the Book of Leviticus* (Downers Grove, Ill.: InterVarsity Press, 2015), 137–40.
3 Warfield, "Fundamental Significance," I.337.

Chapter 7

1 *The Canons and Decrees of the Council of Trent*, trans. H.J. Schroeder (Charlotte, N.C.: TAN, 2011), 147.
2 *Council of Trent*, 147–48.
3 *Council of Trent*, 151.
4 Martin Luther, "The Babylonian Captivity of the Church," in *Luther's Works*, vol. 36, *Word and Sacrament II*, ed. Abdel Ross Wentz (Philadelphia: Fortress, 1959), 35.
5 Luther, "The Babylonian Captivity of the Church," 36:38–39.
6 Huldrych Zwingli, "The Sixty-Seven Articles," in James T. Dennison, *Reformed Confessions of the 16th and 17th Centuries in English Translation*, vol. 1, *1523–1552* (Grand Rapids, Mich.: Reformation Heritage, 2008), 4.
7 John Calvin, *Institutes of the Christian Religion*, ed. John T. McNeill, trans. Ford Lewis Battles (Philadelphia: Westminster, 1960), 4.18.1.
8 R.P.C. Hanson, *Eucharistic Offering in the Early Church*, Grove Liturgical Study No. 19 (Bramcote, England: Grove, 1979), 17.

9   Warfield, "Fundamental Significance," I.332–8.

Chapter 8

1   Most commentators observe that the phrase "fruit of the vine" was a common Jewish way of speaking of wine, and since wine was the drink used at the Passover, there is no reason to suppose that Jesus was using the phrase to mean anything else.

2   See Robert Letham, *The Lord's Supper* (Phillipsburg, N.J.: P&R, 2001), 54.

3   Walter Bauer, *Greek-English Lexicon of the New Testament and Other Early Christian Literature*, 2nd ed., eds. William F. Arndt, F. Wilbur Gingrich, and Frederick W. Danker (Chicago: University of Chicago Press, 1979), 562; cf. R.V. Pierard, "Alcohol, Drinking of," in *Evangelical Dictionary of Theology*, ed. Walter Elwell (Grand Rapids, Mich.: Baker, 1984), 28; and "Wine" in *Eerdmans Bible Dictionary*, ed. Allen C. Myers (Grand Rapids, Mich.: Eerdmans, 1987), 1058.

4   See the Augsburg Confession, article 10; the Thirty-Nine Articles, article 28; the Dordrecht Confession of Faith, article 10.

5   See the Belgic Confession, article 35; Heidelberg Catechism 79; the Second Helvetic Confession, chapter 19; the Westminster Confession of Faith, 29.3; Westminster Larger Catechism 168, 169, 177.

6   See the 1689 London Baptist Confession of Faith, 30.3; the 1859 Southern Baptist Abstract of Principles; the 1925 Baptist Faith and Message.

Chapter 9

1   Cited by Harold M. Daniels, *To God Alone Be Glory* (Louisville, Ky.: Geneva, 2003), 97.

Chapter 11

1   The word *paedo* means "child." *Paedocommunion*, therefore, means "child-communion."

2   Cornelis Venema, *Children at the Lord's Table?* (Grand Rapids, Mich.: Reformation Heritage, 2009), 3.

3   Venema, *Children at the Lord's Table?*, 3.

SCRIPTURE INDEX

SCRIPTURE INDEX

ABOUT THE AUTHOR

Dr. Keith A. Mathison is professor of systematic theology at Reformation Bible College in Sanford, Fla. He served as an associate editor for the *Reformation Study Bible* and formerly served as an associate editor of *Tabletalk* magazine.

Dr. Mathison has degrees from Houston Baptist University (B.A.), Reformed Theological Seminary (M.A.), and Whitefield Theological Seminary (Ph.D.). He is author of several books, including *The Shape of Sola Scriptura, Given for You: Reclaiming Calvin's Doctrine of the Lord's Supper, From Age to Age: The Unfolding of Biblical Eschatology*, and, with Dr. R.C. Sproul, *Not a Chance: God, Science, and the Revolt against Reason.*